Rebbe Yisrael, the Maggid of Kozhnitz

Rebbe Menachem Mendel of Rimanov

Rebbe Yaakov Yitzchak, the Chozeh of Lublin

Rebbe Avraham Yehoshua Heschel of Apta

A SHAAR PRESS PUBLICATION

FOUR CHASSIDIC MASTERS

The Heart, the Mind, the Eye, and the Tongue —
History, Stories, Teachings

RABBI ABRAHAM J. TWERSKI, M.D.

© Copyright 2008 by Shaar Press

First Edition – First Impression / November 2008

Published by **SHAAR PRESS**
Distributed by MESORAH PUBLICATIONS, LTD.
4401 Second Avenue / Brooklyn, N.Y 11232 / (718) 921-9000

ALL RIGHTS RESERVED

No part of this book may be reproduced **in any form,** photocopy, electronic media, or otherwise without **written** permission from the copyright holder, except by a reviewer who wishes to quote brief passages in connection with a review written for inclusion in magazines or newspapers.
THE RIGHTS OF THE COPYRIGHT HOLDER WILL BE STRICTLY ENFORCED.

ISBN 10: 1-42260-874-3
ISBN 13: 978-1-42260-874-6

Printed in the United States of America by Noble Book Press

Table of Contents

Preface	7
Introduction	9
Rebbe Yisrael Haupstein the Maggid of Kozhnitz (1737-1814)	63
Rebbe Menachem Mendel of Rimanov (1745-1815) & Rebbe Tzvi Hirsch HaKohen (1778-1847)	91
Rebbe Yaakov Yitzchak HaLevi Horowitz the Chozeh ("Seer") of Lublin (1747–1815)	149
Rebbe Avraham Yehoshua Heschel of Apta (1748–1825)	197

Preface

After the demise of Rebbe Reb Elimelech of Lizhensk, his disciples asked his brother, Rebbe Reb Zusia of Anipole, to assume the mantle of leadership. Rebbe Reb Zusia cited the verse (*Genesis* 2:10) "And a river went forth from Eden to water the garden, and from there it separated into four principal streams." "Eden" refers to the Baal Shem Tov; "river" refers to his disciple, Rebbe DovBer of Mezeritch; "garden" is my brother, the *Noam Elimelech*; and from *Noam Elimelech* flow four principal streams: the Rebbe of Lublin, the Maggid of Kozhnitz, the Rebbe of Rimanov, and the Rebbe of Apta. These four great Chassidic masters serve as role models for their time — and for ours.

Introduction

It is with great trepidation that I write this book. I hesitate to identify myself as a fool, although it is said, "Fools rush in where angels fear to tread." How foolish it is to even attempt to depict spiritual giants the mention of whose names sends chills through my body! Yet, everything that G-d created has a purpose, and perhaps the *purpose* of folly is that it can give one the courage to undertake projects that wiser people would avoid.

Growing up in a Chassidic family and with a heritage of the great Chassidic masters, I was immersed in stories about these *tzaddikim* and many of their Torah teachings. While one cannot vouch for the veracity of all the anecdotes, the very fact that these stories are told is a testimony to the masters.

My dear friend, Rabbi Berel Wein, relates the incident wherein the Chofetz Chaim was called to testify in court as a character witness, and said that he could not take the oath because in his entire life he had avoided swearing to anything. The attorney explained to the judge that it was not necessary to swear in this witness.

Attempting to describe the saintliness of the Chofetz Chaim, the attorney said, "This rabbi once saw a thief making off with his candlesticks. He promptly divested himself of their ownership so that the thief should not be guilty of theft."

The judge said, "Do you expect me to believe that?"

The attorney replied, "Your Honor, people do not tell stories like that about me or you."

The kind of stories that are told about people is an indication of who they are.

I was privileged to hear first-person stories. I knew people who knew the *tzaddikim* of Sanz and Cherkassy. My parents and grandparents personally knew the *tzaddikim* about whom these stories are told, and I heard several miraculous incidents recounted by eyewitnesses.

My attitude is that expressed by the Rebbe of Satmar in regard to stories about the Baal Shem Tov. He said, "Anyone who believes that all these stories are true is credulous. Anyone who thinks that they could not have happened is a heretic."

Stories of *tzaddikim,* ancient and contemporary, abound. Some people claim that portraying *tzaddikim* as superhuman beings does not inspire anyone, because their spirituality is far beyond our reach. These critics are missing the point. Leaving the concert hall following a performance by the great violinist Pinhas Zukerman, I heard a father say to his son, "Do you think you will ever play the violin like that?" The child said, "No, but now that I know what 'perfect' is, I'll practice an extra half-hour every day."

True, the saintliness of these *tzaddikim* is far beyond our reach, but perhaps, like the child, we will make an effort to "practice an extra half-hour every day."

Are some of the stories fabricated? Perhaps. But we are not talking about ancient history. In Canada in 1927, my father met a man, 114 years old, who had seen Rebbe Mordechai of Chernoble (the Maggid of Chernoble), a Chassidic luminary. He was a man of 24 when the Maggid died. The anecdotal information that has been recorded about the *tzaddikim* is voluminous, and if only a fraction of the tales is true, their actions are most impressive.

The importance of stories about *tzaddikim* can be appreciated from the fact that Hagaon Rav Baruch Ber Lebovitz would relate to his students the greatness of *tzaddikim* that he knew, as did his master, Reb Chaim of Brisk. Reb Baruch Ber would tearfully say, "Oh! If only you had merited seeing the *yiras Shamayim* of the Rebbe." These Torah giants, who never allowed a moment to pass without Torah study, felt that relating tales about the lives and deeds of *tzaddikim* was as important as Torah study Indeed, Rashi (*Genesis* 24:42) quotes the Midrash stating that the conversation of the servants of the Patriarchs is superior to the Torah of their descendants. The account of how *tzaddikim* lived their lives is a practical guide to the implementation of the Torah in our lives.

Meiri (*Yoma* 38b) says that it is a mitzvah to relate the praises of *tzaddikim*, because it encourages people to emulate them. This is also stated by Ramchal in *Mesilas Yesharim*, Chapter 21.

The power of a story can best be illustrated — by a story!

☞ Rebbe Yisrael of Rhizin related that when the Baal Shem Tov saw that misfortune was threatening to befall *Klal Yisrael*, he would go to a particular place in the woods to meditate. He lit a candle and said prayers with certain kabbalistic *kavannos* (meditations), and the misfortune was averted.

Later, the Baal Shem Tov's successor, Rebbe DovBer, the Maggid of Mezeritch, had occasion to intercede in heaven to abrogate an unfavorable decree. He would go to the same place in the woods, and say "*Ribono shel Olam* [Master of the Universe], I can light the candle and say a prayer, but I do not know the *kavannos.*" This, too, averted the decree.

Later yet, Rebbe Moshe Leib of Sassov said, "*Ribono shel Olam,* I do not know the prayer, but I know the place, and I can light a candle there. May the merit of the *tzaddikim* who prayed here arouse Your mercy on Your people."

The Rebbe of Rizhin would say, "*Ribono shel Olam,* I do not know the prayer, I do not know the *kavannos,* and I do not even know the place. All I can do is to relate what these *tzaddikim* did, and may their merit bring us salvation."

Stories about *tzaddikim* can elicit great *chesed* (kindness) from Hashem.

I chose to write about these four *tzaddikim* because, although they were all disciples of one teacher, each one exemplified a particular attribute. While alike in many respects, they were unique individuals. In a culture that worships equality, and in an educational system that fosters sameness rather than individuality, it is important to stress that we are indeed as unique as our fingerprints. The Midrash says, "Just as people's facial features are dissimilar, so are their minds dissimilar" (*Tanchuma Pinchas* 10). The uniqueness of each person should be appreciated by parents, teachers, and individuals. While it is true that we may not be close to greatness as were these *tzaddikim,* we can each be ourselves.

I have written several books about self-esteem, which simply means having a valid self-awareness. My experience tells me that most people do not know their true selves, although they firmly believe that they do.

We are not expected to be as great as these *tzaddikim*. We are only expected to be as great as we can be. Alas! So many of us fall short of that goal.

Each of these four *tzaddikim* worked to perfect his uniqueness. All that is asked is that we work toward perfecting our uniqueness.

≥§ *The Birth of Chassidism*

One of the strengths of Jewish survival is the respect for tradition. Anything new is looked upon with suspicion. This was best expressed by R' Moshe Schreiber (author of *Chasam Sofer*), who applied a halachic statement to any innovation in Yiddishkeit. There is a halachah that *chadash,* the new crop of grain, may not be eaten until after the offering of the *Omer* (*Leviticus* 23:9-14), hence the expression *chadash assur min haTorah* — new (grain) is forbidden by the Torah. The Chasam Sofer used this phrase to express the idea that *anything* new is forbidden by the Torah.

In the 17th century, the debacle of Shabbatai Zvi, the false messiah, elevated fear of any innovation to a new height, almost to paranoia. Ramchal, one of the greatest Torah personalities in Jewish history, was hounded and almost placed under a *cherem* (ban). The Baal Shem Tov's novel approach to *avodas Hashem* (service of Hashem) met with fierce opposition. Even the *mussar* movement launched by Rebbe Yisrael of Salant had to withstand condemnation.

The acid test of legitimate Yiddishkeit was proposed by Moses during the Korach rebellion. "In the morrow Hashem will make known who is His own" (*Numbers* 16:5); i.e., the future will tell. The innovations that endure are legitimate Yiddishkeit. The Sadducees were once a powerful sect, but are extinct. Chassidism and devotees of the *mussar* movement are very much alive today.

❧ *Baal Shem Tov*

The Chassidic movement was launched by the Baal Shem Tov, R' Yisrael ben Eliezer of Okup (5460–5520 [1700–1760]), at a time when Jews in Russia and Poland were severely oppressed, living under anti-Semitic governments, among an anti-Semitic citizenry. Jews were not permitted to live in large cities, and dwelled in villages and hamlets, barely eking out a living. Many sources of income were closed to them, and pogroms were common. The Jews still suffered, physically from the devastation of the Chmelnicki massacre, and spiritually from the bitter disillusionment of the Shabbatai Zvi debacle. Many had been unable to receive a Torah education, sometimes having no more than basic knowledge of *Chumash* (Pentateuch) or even just the ability to read the *siddur* (prayerbook).

The Baal Shem Tov's mission was to enable these oppressed people to experience the *simchah* (joy) of being Jews, to know that Hashem loves them, and to discover that even those who were not Torah scholars could be dedicated and devoted to Hashem. The motto of Chassidism was *Rachmana libbe ba'i* — the Merciful One (Hashem) desires the devotion of the heart.

When the Baal Shem Tov heard a *maggid* (itinerant preacher) rebuking the people for what he felt was laxity in observance of Torah, he said, "Do you not realize — when a Jew comes home, exhausted from a hard day's work, and says, '*Oy!* It's just a few minutes before sundown,' and quickly prays Minchah [the afternoon service] — do you not realize that the heavenly angels tremble from the holiness of that prayer?"

The Baal Shem Tov emphasized *ahavas Hashem* (love for G-d) and *ahavas Yisrael* (love of fellow Jews). When asked how one can develop love for Hashem, since He is beyond the grasp of the senses, the Baal Shem said, "Love your fellow Jews; this will lead to love for Hashem."

The Baal Shem Tov welcomed and showed much devotion to the simple folk. At one *shalosh seudos* (the third meal of Shabbos), the Baal Shem Tov was expounding deep secrets of the Torah to his disciples. R' DovBer, the Maggid of Mezeritch, who was to become the Baal Shem Tov's successor, thought, "How fortunate we are to be able to hear these profound Torah discourses from the Master, not like the simple folk in the anteroom who know nothing beyond the *siddur*."

The Baal Shem Tov told his disciples to place their arms on their neighbors' shoulders. He then placed his arms on the shoulders of the two disciples closest to him, closing the circle. The Maggid said that he felt transported to the heights of Heaven, where he heard recitation of heartrending verses of *Tehillim* (*Psalms*). One was, "O, Heavenly Father, I seek You. My soul thirsts for You, my flesh longs for You" (*Psalms* 63:2). Another voice pleaded, "My soul yearns, indeed it pines, for the courtyards of Hashem" (ibid. 84:3).

The sweet chanting of the verses moved the Maggid to tears, and he thought, "If only I could achieve that intense love for Hashem."

The Baal Shem Tov then removed his arms from the disciples' shoulders and said, "The verses you heard in Heaven were those being recited by the simple folk in the anteroom."

Some great Torah personalities, including the Gaon of Vilna, feared that a popular movement led by a charismatic leader who taught *kabbalah* was too reminiscent of what had happened several decades earlier with Shabbatai Zvi, and they vigorously opposed the Chassidic movement. However, the Chassidic movement increased in strength and spread widely through Russia and Poland.

Chassidism stressed the immanence of the *Shechinah* (Divine Presence) and the awareness that every Jew possesses a *neshamah* (soul) that is not only G-dly, but is actual G-dliness. The Torah states that man was created when Hashem blew a breath of life into his nostrils (*Genesis* 2:7); the *Zohar* points out that when one exhales, he breathes out something from within himself. Hence, when Hashem "blew" the *neshamah* into man, He blew from within Himself; man's *neshamah* is, therefore, formed by the essence of Hashem.

The renowned chassid, R' Hillel of Paritsch, once noticed a person weeping after *davening*. Thinking that there might be something that he could do to help, R' Hillel inquired why he was crying.

The man said, "I am crying out of sympathy for my *neshamah*. It is part of Hashem Himself, so holy and pure, but it is trapped within an earthly body that craves so many things that are anathema to the *neshamah*. How the *neshamah* must be suffering!"

Yet the awareness that one has a Divine *neshamah* that enables a person to be in intimate contact with Hashem is cause for great joy. Due to the Baal Shem Tov, Jews who were impoverished and oppressed could nevertheless sing and dance.

Volumes have been written about the Baal Shem Tov, and I cannot possibly duplicate them here. Perhaps we can grasp an idea of the Baal Shem Tov's essence from the comment made by his successor, the Maggid of Mezeritch, who said, "I am exhilarated when I see R' Zvi, the son of the Baal Shem Tov, because that makes me aware that he was actually a human being, not a *seraph*."

Teachings

The Talmud says, "Who is wise? One who learns from every person" (*Ethics of the Fathers* 4:1). But can every person be a teacher? The answer is that when one is in the presence of a *tzaddik*, he should learn what he must do. When one is in the presence of a *rasha*, he must learn what *not* to do.

"For a sun and a shield is Hashem" (*Psalms* 84:12). One cannot look at the sun without using a screen. Similarly, Hashem enclosed and concealed His light within "screens" (*tzimtzum haShechinah* — "contraction" of the Divine light).

Rashi says that there was an initial light of creation, but because the wicked did not deserve to benefit from this light, Hashem concealed it for the *tzaddikim* in the future, and created a second light (*Genesis* 1:4). The Midrash says that the initial light enabled a person to see from one end of the world to the other. Where did Hashem conceal the initial light? In the Torah, and through the Torah, one can see from one end of the world to the other.

"Hashem is your shadow at your right hand" (*Psalms* 121:5). The shadow mimics one's every move. If one raises his hand, the hand of the shadow is raised. Thus, Hashem "mimics" a person's behavior.

If a person gives *tzeddakah* even to people who are not deserving, Hashem will give to him even if he is undeserving.

> Rebbe Reb Zusia of Anipole had a chassid who would give him money from time to time, and the chassid prospered. Once, when the chassid came to Reb Zusia, he was told that Reb Zusia had gone to his Rebbe, the Maggid of Mezeritch. The chassid said, "If the Maggid of Mezeritch is Rebbe Zusia's Rebbe, then he must be greater than Rebbe Zusia," and instead of giving money to Rebbe Zusia, he gave it to the Maggid.
>
> His business began to fail. He asked Rebbe Zusia why this had happened, and Rebbe Zusia said, "When you did not discriminate and gave to Zusia even though he was not deserving, then Hashem did not discriminate and gave to you. But when you sought to give only to a great *tzaddik*, Hashem also decided to give only to a great *tzaddik*, and you did not qualify."

Why do we say, "our G-d and G-d of our forefathers?" Because there are two types of faith: 1. By tradition, transmitted from father to son, and 2. By reasoning to the realization that there is one true G-d. The first is not subject to refutation by logical argument, but it is a superficial faith. The second has the strength of conviction, but is subject to being disproved by logical argument. Therefore, we should have both types of faith; hence we say, "*our* G-d *and* G-d of our forefathers."

A poor person's contact with Hashem surpasses that of a wealthy person, because the poor man consistently prays to Hashem, whereas a wealthy person can afford to pray periodically. Similarly, Hashem attends to the poor person every day, whereas He attends to the wealthy person only periodically.

Hashem cursed the serpent, "Dust shall you eat all the days of your life" (*Genesis* 3:14). How is that a curse? The serpent will have an endless supply of food. But Hashem said, "All other living things must turn to Me for their sustenance, but you are so despicable that I never wish to hear from you."

☞ A cruelly anti-Semitic decree was promulgated, and a fast day was declared. People gathered in shul, and they wept while praying. A woman who could not read the *siddur* was very moved, and said, "Master of the Universe! You are a merciful Father. I have five children, and if I do not have food for them and they cry, my soul goes out to them in great anguish. And You, our heavenly Father, so many of Your children are crying to You and pleading for Your help. Why, even if You had a heart of stone it would melt!"

The Baal Shem Tov said, "It was this woman's prayer that resulted in the decree being revoked."

Regardless how sinful Jews may be, Hashem remains with them, as the Torah says, "Who dwells with them amid their contamination" (*Leviticus* 16:16). However, if a person is vain, Hashem says, "He and I cannot dwell together" (*Arachin* 15:2).

Vanity results in sadness, because the person thinks, "I am not receiving that to which I am entitled."

Why is it necessary to go to a *tzaddik*? One can learn proper *middos* and conduct by studying *mussar* writings. The Torah says, "Hashem said to Moses, 'Write this as a remembrance in the Book and recite it in the ears of Joshua'" (*Exodus* 17:14). Obviously, the fact that it is in a book is not enough. Personal contact is essential.

☞ A man complained to the Baal Shem Tov, "I've put in a great deal of effort to improve my *avodas Hashem* (service of G-d), but I feel I haven't accomplished anything."

The Baal Shem Tov said, "You have accomplished a great deal. You have achieved humility."

"Praiseworthy is the man to whom Hashem does not ascribe iniquity" (*Psalms* 32:2). If we add a comma, the verse can be read, "Praiseworthy is the man, who, when he does not think of Hashem, considers that to be inquity."

A person (i.e., *kohen*) can look at all lesions except at his own" (*Negaim* 2:5). This can also be read as כָּל הַנְּגָעִים אָדָם רוֹאֶה, חוּץ מִנִּגְעֵי עַצְמוֹ — All the defects that a person sees outside of himself are due to his own defects. The Baal Shem Tov taught that when we see a fault in another person, we should examine our character traits, because we, ourselves, must have that fault."

☞ The Baal Shem Tov chanced to see someone violating Shabbos. Following his own teaching, he did a soul-searching to find where he himself had violated Shabbos. When he could not find a violation of Shabbos, he prayed that his transgression should be revealed to him. It was revealed to him that he had heard someone insulting a *tzaddik*, and he did not rebuke the person. Inasmuch as the *Zohar* says that a *tzaddik* has the *kedushah* of Shabbos, this was tantamount to a violation of Shabbos.

~§ *Rebbe DovBer of Mezeritch (5464-5533[1704-1773])*

The Maggid of Mezeritch, Rebbe DovBer, was a great Torah scholar, having studied Torah with the author of *Pnei Yehoshua*. He was accomplished in *kabbalah*, and when he heard of the Baal Shem Tov, he decided to see for himself whether the accounts were true.

Upon meeting the Baal Shem Tov, the Maggid expected to hear profound teachings, but the Baal Shem Tov only told him that once he had driven through the wilderness for days and had no bread to feed his coachman, until a peasant happened along and sold him some bread. He then dismissed the Maggid.

On the next day, the Maggid again visited the Baal Shem Tov with the expectation of hearing his teachings, but again the Baal Shem Tov told him that once, when he was on the road, he had no hay for his horses. A farmer came along and gave him some hay.

The Maggid was convinced that all he had heard about the greatness of the Baal Shem Tov was false, and decided that the next morning he would return home. Around midnight, he received a message that the Baal Shem Tov wanted to see him. The Baal Shem Tov received him in his room and said, "Are you well versed in *kabbalah*?" The Maggid said that he was. The Baal Shem Tov gave him the *Pri Etz Chaim* (*The Fruit of the Tree of Life*, written by the Arizal's disciple, R' Chaim Vital).

"Read!" the Baal Shem Tov said, and the Maggid read.

"Expound!" the Baal Shem Tov said, and the Maggid expounded on a passage that dealt with the nature of angels.

"Get up!" the Baal Shem Tov said, and the Maggid stood up.

The Baal Shem Tov then read the same passage. Suddenly, the room was aflame with dazzling light, and the Maggid fainted.

When he recovered, the Baal Shem Tov said, "You expounded correctly, but your knowledge of *kabbalah* lacks the *neshamah* of *kabbalah*." The Baal Shem Tov explained the hidden messages in what he had said about the coachman and the horses. The Maggid remained with the Baal Shem Tov, and eventually became his successor.

> When the Maggid was a child, a fire destroyed his home. His mother wept, saying, "I'm not crying about the house. The document of our *yichus* [genealogy], generation after generation of great Torah scholars and *tzaddikim*, is gone."
>
> The child said, "Don't cry, Mother. A new *yichus* will begin with me."
>
> The Maggid's great-grandson, Rebbe Yisrael, was the father of the Rizhin dynasty.

The Maggid gathered about him many disciples, including Rebbe Elimelech of Lizhensk and the four subjects of this book. Among his disciples were outstanding Torah giants such as Rebbe Shmelke of Nikolsburg; his brother, Rebbe Pinchas, author of the Talmudic classic, *Haflaah*; and Rebbe Shneur Zalman of Liadi, author of *Tanya* and the *Shulchan Aruch HaRav.* Their enormous Torah erudition can be seen in their writings. Rebbi Levi Yitzchak of Berditchev, Rebbe Menachem Mendel of Vitebsk, Rebbe Zusia of Anipole, and Rebbe

Ahron of Karlin were among the Maggid's disciples.

☞ One Friday afternoon, as the Maggid was resting, he called in a disciple. "Go find Zusia," he said, "and tell him to stop reciting *Shir HaShirim* [Song of Songs]. He is causing such a furor in Heaven that it disturbs my sleep."

☞ My father related an interesting story about the Maggid and Rebbe Aharon of Karlin. Rebbe Aharon came to receive a *berachah* from the Maggid before going home for *Pesach*. The Maggid blessed him, saying, "*Fohr gezunderheit*" (have a safe trip), but after he left, the Maggid sent several of his peers to bring him back. When he returned, the Maggid again blessed him, and again sent men to bring him back. This was repeated three times.

Ultimately, Rebbe Aharon left for home; he passed away on Chol Hamoed *Pesach*, The Maggid's disciples understood why he had been called back, and realized that had he remained there, he would not have died. They were extremely fond of Rebbe Aharon, and they said, "If the Master had only told us, we would have tied him in chains to keep him here."

The Maggid said, "Hashem said of Moses, 'In My entire house he is the trusted one' (*Numbers* 12:7). What does it mean that Moses was trusted? There was nothing to steal there. 'Trusted' means that he could keep a secret and not reveal what he knew."

☞ The Maggid once told his disciples that a *neshamah* from a very lofty spiritual realm was destined to come down to the world. He told Rebbe Nachum of Chernoble to visit the grave of

Rebbe Aharon and tell him that the Maggid promised that the bearer of this *neshamah* would marry Rebbe Aharon's orphaned daughter. That year, Rebbe Mordechai of Chernoble was born, and indeed married Rebbe Aharon's daughter.

At the *tenaim* (engagement), Rebbe Menachem Mendel of Vitebsk was given the text of the *tenaim* (betrothal document) to read aloud, and when he came to the words, "… and the one who stands at the side of his daughter, the *kallah,* is Rebbe Aharon," Rebbe Menachem Mendel fainted.

The Maggid revived him and asked, "What happened? Were you surprised to see our Rebbe Aharon?"

Rebbe Menachem Mendel said, "No, it's just that I was unaware that in so short a time he had become so great" (Rebbe Aharon died at a young age).

The Maggid shrugged. "Levi Yitzchak [of Berditchev] sees more than you and he doesn't faint."

The third son resulting from the marriage of Rebbe Mordechai of Chernoble and the daughter of Rebbe Aharon was my ancestor, Rebbe Yaakov Yisrael of Cherkassy, who is known to us as "the Cherkassy Zeide."[1]

The Maggid had one son, Rebbe Avraham the *Malach* (angel). After the Maggid's death, the disciples wanted Rebbe Avraham to succeed his father in the leadership, but he refused.

When the misnagdim (the opponents of Chassidism) pronounced a *cherem* on the chassidim, several of the Maggid's disciples

---
1. More about the Cherkassy Zeide can be found in my book, *The Zeide Reb Motele* (Mesorah Publications, 2002).

responded by pronouncing a *cherem* on the misnagdim. When the Maggid heard of this, he was very upset. He said, "What you have accomplished in the conflict with the misnagdim is that you will be triumphant, but you have lost your leader." That year, the Maggid died.

On the day before his death, the Maggid said to his disciples, "My children, let there be unity among you, and you will overcome everything."

The Maggid lay silent for a long time, but his lips were moving. Rebbe Zusia of Anipole entered the room quietly, and the Maggid opened his eyes.

"Who came in?" he asked.

Rebbe Shneur Zalman said, "Zusia came in." The Maggid motioned for Rebbe Zusia to approach. He put his left hand on Rebbe Zusia's right hand and said, "You were mine in this world, and in the eternal world you will be together with me."

The Maggid closed his eyes for a while, then awoke and said, "Where is Menachem Mendel [of Vitebsk]?"

Rebbe Shneur Zalman said, "Menachem Mendel is not here."

"And is R' Yehudah Leib HaKohen here?" the Maggid asked.

Rebbe Shneur Zalman said, "R' Yehudah Leib HaKohen is here." R' Yehudah Leib HaKohen approached the bed.

The Maggid said, "Yehudah Leib, you are a *kohen*. 'The lips of a *kohen* should safeguard knowledge' [*Malachi* 2:7]. You will be together with me."

The Maggid then turned his gaze to Rebbe Shneur Zalman. "Shneur Zalman," he said, "give me your hand. You will be alone. You will go your own way. You will need very great Heavenly help. I will long for you very much, and with Hashem's help, I will extract you from all your ordeals."

The Maggid then asked, "Where is my son Avraham? I don't see my son Avraham." Avraham, the *Malach*, had been secluded in his room. It was as if he did not exist in this earthly world. He was called to the Maggid's bedside.

"Avraham," his father said, "I have nothing to instruct you. You will not deviate from your holy way. I have just one request, my son. Speak and enlighten people with your words. You have been silent too long." The Maggid kept his gaze on his son, as if expecting a response, but Rebbe Avraham the *Malach* remained silent.

The Maggid then closed his eyes for the last time.

Teachings

A wise person can eat delicacies and be in anguish.

☞ A poor man asked a Rebbe for a *berachah* for prosperity. The Rebbe said, "I will give you a *berachah* on condition that you follow my instructions without deviating." The man promised to obey.

The Rebbe gave him a sum of money. "Go buy the finest delicacies, take them home, and eat them in the presence of your children. Under no circumstances are you to give them even a tiny morsel of the food. Then come back to me."

The man brought the food home, and when the children smelled the aroma, they were thrilled, expecting to be fed. The man sat down in the presence of his children and began eating.

The hungry children watched him, and their mouths watered. Seeing his hungry children craving food and not being able to share it with them, he choked on every bite. It would have been easier for him to eat rocks.

When he returned to the Rebbe, the latter said, "If you will be wealthy, will you be able to enjoy your wealth with the knowledge that there are so many people who are destitute?" The Rebbe then gave him a *berachah*.

The man became wealthy and established a kitchen for the poor. Instead of eating at home, he ate with the poor.

It is actually easier to achieve *ruach hakodesh* in the Diaspora than when the *Beis HaMikdash* existed. This concept is illustrated by the parable of a king who is difficult to reach when in his palace. However, when he leaves the palace and goes through the country, even simple villagers may have access to him. When the *Beis HaMikdash* was destroyed and Jews went into exile, the *Shechinah* accompanied them. Hence, the king is in exile and is more approachable.

We should learn three things from an infant: (1) An infant is never depressed. (2) An infant is never idle. (3) When an infant wants something, he cries until he gets it.

The verse, בִּזְמַן שֶׁאַתֶּם עוֹשִׂין רְצוֹנוֹ שֶׁל מָקוֹם אַתֶּם קְרוּיִן בָּנִים, וּבִזְמַן שֶׁאֵין אַתֶּם עוֹשִׂין רְצוֹנוֹ שֶׁל מָקוֹם אַתֶּם קְרוּיִן עֲבָדִים, is generally translated, "When Israel does Hashem's will, they are called His children, and when Israel does not do Hashem's will, they are called His servants" (*Bava Basra* 10a). But does a servant not do the will of his master? עוֹשִׂין does not mean "do," but rather "make."

The Talmud says that if a *tzaddik* decrees something, Hashem implements it, and a *tzaddik* also has the ability to cancel a Divine decree (*Moed Kattan* 16b). A *tzaddik* thus has the ability to fashion Hashem's will. This is what the Talmud means. When Israel *fashions* Hashem's will, they are considered His children.

Before retiring at night, a person should make an accounting of his actions during the day. If he thinks that because he did good things he is superior to others and he therefore becomes vain, all the good deeds that he did are for nought.

Yiras Shamayim does not mean fear of being punished, but rather a feeling of awe at the Majesty of Hashem. Fear of punishment causes a person to be distant from Hashen, as one runs away from a frightening object. The awareness of Hashem's Majesty gives rise to a desire to be close to Him.

The essence of a person is one's mind, one's ability to think. Wherever one's thoughts are, that's where the person is.

> *Rebbe Mendel of Kotzk applied this concept to teshuvah. One must run away from a sin and not ruminate over it. A sin is like mud. Whatever you do with it, you get dirty. If you think about the sin, then you put yourself into the sin. You are wherever your mind is.*

The Talmud says that the Torah "clothes one with humility" (*Ethics of the Fathers* 6:1). Humility is like a garment. One can wear it or cast it off.

> *The sifrei mussar point out that although anivus (humility) is the most desirable trait, sometimes one must set aside anivus and assert oneself. A classical example is seen in the actions of King Saul. His anivus was profound (I Samuel 10:22), but when he succumbed to the demand of the people to spare the livestock of Amalek, the prophet reprimanded him, "Though you are small in your own eyes, you are the head of the tribes of Israel" (ibid., 15:17).*
>
> *The Talmud says, "The anivus of R' Zachariah ben Avkolos caused the destruction of the Beis HaMikdash" (Gittin 56a). Sometimes, the garment of anivus must be shed.*

וְהָיָה כְּנַגֵּן הַמְנַגֵּן וַתְּהִי עָלָיו יַד ה' is usually translated, "And it was, when the musician played, the spirit of Hashem rested on him" (*II Kings* 3:15). However, it may have an additional meaning. הַמְנַגֵּן is the musician, מְנַגֵּן is the musical instrument. A musician may take pride in his performance. The musical instrument can feel no pride. Thus, if the musician will be as devoid of vanity as the instrument, that will invite the spirit of Hashem.

Similarly, "Lift your voice like the shofar" (*Isaiah* 58:1) is interpreted, "Your prayer should be devoid of personal pride, just as the shofar has no personal interest."

If not for the continuing energy of Hashem, the world would not exist. One who has true spirit can see the word of Hashem in everything.

> *This concept is elaborated in Tanya. Once a craftsman completes an item, it has an independent existence. Not so the world, which was in a state of nothingness before creation. The utterances of Hashem*

> that caused creation continue to sustain the world. Everything in existence has a spark of G-dliness within it that sustains it. If that spark were withdrawn, the object would go out of existence.

A *tzaddik* is someone who is constantly bonded to Hashem.

Some *tzaddikim* are so humble that they do not believe that their prayers warrant being heard; therefore, their prayers accomplish nothing. One should believe that Hashem hears everyone's prayer.

܀ั *The Four Masters*

It is told that when Rebbe Elimelech of Lizhensk (1717–1787) left this world, he bequeathed four of his attributes to four of his disciples. To Rebbe Yisrael of Koznitz he gave the spirit of his heart, to Rebbe Menachem Mendel of Rimanov he bequeathed the soul of his mind, to Rebbe Yaakov Yitzchak of Lublin (the *Chozeh* — Seer) he gave the sight of his eyes, and to Rebbe Avraham Yehoshua Heschel of Apta he gave the power of his speech.

In trying to understand the uniqueness of these four *tzaddikim*, we are overwhelmed by their greatness. It is like looking into four searchlights of a million watts each and trying to distinguish the differences among them. We are blinded by the intensity of the light. However, we have a precedent in Moses, whose face radiated so brightly that he had to wear a mask to enable people to be in his presence (*Exodus* 34:29-35). We must assume that what we see of these *tzaddikim* is only that which has penetrated the mask.

It is particularly difficult to associate any one attribute to any one of the *tzaddikim*. Each one excelled in the spirit of the heart, the soul of the mind, the sight of the eyes, and the power of speech. All I can do is relate whatever we know about these *tzaddikim* and allow the reader to make the proper associations.

Inasmuch as these four *tzaddikim* were disciples of Rebbe Elimelech of Lizhensk, we must say a few words about him. "A few words" is an appropriate expression, because even an entire volume about Rebbe Elimelech would be only "a few words," relative to his incomparable greatness. Chassidim refer to him with the double title, "the Rebbe Reb Melech," an appellation given to only a few Chassidic masters.

In his earlier years Rebbe Elimelech was an outstanding Talmudic scholar. His older brother, Rebbe Zusia of Anipole, a disciple of the Baal Shem Tov's successor, the Maggid of Mezeritch, persuaded Rebbe Elimelech to visit the Maggid; Rebbe Elimelech, too, became a devoted follower. It was through the four disciples that Chassidism was introduced to Poland and Hungary.

> Rebbe Elimelech and his brother, Rebbe Zusia, accepted upon themselves two years of exile to atone for their perceived "sins" and to intensify their spirituality. En route home after the two years, Rebbe Elimelech visited the *tzaddik* Rebbe Mendele of Linsk, who said, "Had I been in exile for two years, I would have achieved a greater spirituality."
>
> When he entered his hometown, Rebbe Elimelech was told that his son, Elazar, was seriously ill. Rebbe Elimelech rushed home and asked his wife, "What is wrong with Elazar?"
>
> She responded, "Nothing is wrong with Elazar. He is in *cheder.*"

"But I was told that Elazar is seriously ill," he said.

His wife said, "Another child in the neighborhood named Elazar is sick."

Rebbe Elimelech breathed a sigh of relief, but immediately thereafter said to himself, "So, Elimelech, after two years of exile there is still a difference to you whether it is *your* Elazar or someone else's Elazar? Rebbe Mendele was right!" He promptly departed to spend another year in exile.

Rebbe Elimelech said that he was assured of entering *Gan Eden* (Paradise). "When the Heavenly Tribunal asks, 'Did you learn Torah properly?' I will say, 'No.' 'Did you fulfill the mitzvos properly?' I will say, 'No.' 'Did you give adequate *tzeddakah*?' I will say, 'No.' The Tribunal will say, "He speaks the truth. He deserves *Gan Eden*."

On another occasion, Rebbe Elimelech said, "The Sages tell us that Hashem fulfills all the mitzvos of the Torah. How can Hashem fulfill the mitzvah of *tzeddakah* in the World to Come, where there is no eating or drinking and no physical needs? Hashem will fulfill the mitzvah of *tzeddakah* by rewarding people like Melech, who are undeserving of reward, with *Gan Eden*."

Rebbe Elimelech often held forth on the overwhelming importance of truth and the gravity of the sin of falsehood. Even an unintentional lie is a serious sin, he said. On the other hand, the merit of truth is so great that if a person did not utter a single falsehood for an entire 24-hour period, one is assured of *Gan Eden* even if one was otherwise a *rasha* (sinner).

⤳ One chassid, R' Avraham, felt that this was a bargain of which he had to take advantage. He secluded himself in a room, locked the door, and told his family that he was not to be disturbed. He put on his *tallis* and *tefillin* and studied Torah all day. He forced himself to stay awake all night, lest he might talk in his sleep.

Before dawn, there was a loud knock at the door. Not wanting his family to be awakened, he answered the door. It was a neighbor, who said, "Give me the axe. I need the axe."

R' Avraham said, "I'm sorry, but I don't have your axe."

"You lie," the man said. "Yesterday, I was hungry, but I had no money, so I asked your wife to lend me some money. As a pledge, I left her my axe. Here is the money I borrowed; now give me my axe."

R' Avraham was heartbroken because his attempt to avoid a falsehood had failed. He went to Rebbe Elimelech, who greeted him warmly.

"It was the axe, the axe!" R' Avraham cried.

R' Elimelech said, "Sometimes an unintentional sin occurs to teach you something. There is little merit in being truthful when one has secluded oneself from the world. We do not believe in isolating ourselves. We must observe the mitzvos while leading a normal life, interacting with others. If a person interacts normally with other people and is careful not to say a falsehood for 24 hours, *that* is meritorious.

"The incident with the axe occurred to teach you this principle," Rebbe Elimelech concluded.

Kankan HaKesef, Vol. 1

Rebbe Elimelech's humility is legendary. Rebbe Shneur Zalman of Liadi (author of *Tanya*) once visited a *talmid chacham* (Torah scholar) who opposed the Chassidic movement. The scholar pointed to the *sefer Noam Elimelech*, which contains Rebbe Elimelech's teachings, and which the scholar, as an act of denigration, had thrown under a chair. Derisively, he said to Rebbe Shneur Zalman, "What can you tell me about the author of that *sefer*?"

Rebbe Shneur Zalman replied, "I can tell you that if you had thrown the author himself under a chair, he would not have reacted."

In my writings on self-esteem, I have pointed out that awareness of one's character strengths and the degree of one's spirituality is not incompatible with humility. *Tzaddikim* who were aware of their enormous stature did not think themselves superior to or more deserving than others.

This is borne out by the following charming story.

⁌ One Friday, Rebbe Elimelech was in the bathhouse, immersing himself in the *mikveh* in preparation for Shabbos, when a stranger joined him. Rebbe Elimelech engaged him in a conversation. "From where have you come?" he asked.

The man responded, "I am from Hungary, and I came here to see the radiant face of the great *tzaddik*, Rebbe Elimelech."

"And have you seen Melech yet?" Rebbe Elimelech asked.

The man said angrily, "Watch your tongue! How dare you speak disrespectfully about this holy *tzaddik*, the greatest *tzaddik* of this generation! His name is not Melech, but Rebbe Elimelech, may Hashem give him long life."

Rebbe Elimelech said, "So, the falsehood has spread even to Hungary, that Melech, the liar, cheat, and sinner, is thought to be a *tzaddik*."

"Close your mouth, you scoundrel! You are speaking of a Divine angel. If I could, I'd rip you apart for your chutzpah."

After bathing, the man went to his lodging, put on his Shabbos clothes, reviewed the Torah *parashah*, then went to Rebbe Elimelech's home. When he saw Rebbe Elimelech, he was shocked and began to tremble violently.

"Why are you trembling so?" Rebbe Elimelech asked.

"Woe is me!" the man said. "I insulted a G-dly person. I did not know in whose presence I was."

Rebbe Elimelech consoled him. "Don't fret," he said. "What I said about Melech and what you said to Melech in the bathhouse — both of us spoke the truth."

> *This seems contradictory. Rebbe Elimelech agreed that he was both a great tzaddik and sinful. Can these statements be reconciled?*
>
> *The Torah states that Moses was the most humble person ever to be on the earth (Numbers 12:3). Moses' knowledge that he was the only human being ever to speak directly to Hashem did not preclude his being humble. Moses knew his extraordinary powers. He knew that if he would command the earth to open beneath Korach, it would do so (Numbers 16:30). This, too, did not interfere with his humility.*
>
> *Rebbe Yisrael of Salant said, "I know that my mind is equal to a thousand others; that only makes my obligations a thousand times greater."*

☞ One of Rebbe Elimelech's disciples overheard the Rebbe denouncing himself. He said, "How can the Master say things about himself that are untrue?"

Rebbe Elimelech answered, "A king wanted to build himself a new palace, with all new furnishings and appurtenances. One of the peasants who was digging the foundation of the palace had a grudge against the king, and intentionally dug six meters in the wrong direction. When this was discovered, he was given ten lashes and made to fill the ditch and dig in the right place.

"The jeweler who fashioned the diamond that was to be the centerpiece of the crown was a bit negligent and erred $1/10$ of a millimeter in cutting the stone. He was given a severe punishment and dismissed.

"The jeweler's unintentional deviation was $1/60{,}000$ that of the peasant, yet his punishment was much more severe. Why? Because when one is working with the centerpiece of the crown, there is no tolerance for even the slightest deviation."

Because Rebbe Elimelech was aware of his stature, he felt an infinitesimally small dereliction to be that much greater.

Rebbe Elimelech venerated his disciples. The *Chozeh* of Lublin and the Rebbe of Apta regularly came to Lizhensk for Simchas Torah. One year, they did not come, and Rebbe Elimelech was downcast. His son, Rebbe Elazar, asked, "Why is Father so downcast? There are many other *tzaddikim* here."

Rebbe Elimelech said, "My child, none of the other *tzaddikim* are like them. When I build the celestial *Beis HaMikdash,* these two will bring in the Holy Ark and the Tablets when we recite, 'And it was when the Ark would journey'" (*Numbers* 10:35).

To people who sought his advice for *teshuvah*, Rebbe Elimelech spoke in a fatherly manner. By helping them recognize the gravity of a sin and the purity of the *neshamos* for which they must care, he helped them achieve *teshuvah*. Rebbe Elimelech said that learning two pages of Talmud with the commentary of Rosh (Rabbeinu Asher) is of greater value than fasting.

Perhaps the best insight we can have into Rebbe Elimelech is by reading his *Tefillah kodem HaTefillah* (Prayer before praying).

Introductory Prayer of Rebbe Elimelech of Lizhensk

May it be Your will, Hashem, our G-d and G-d of our forefathers, Who listens to the voice of the prayerful entreaties, and hears the voice of His nation Israel with His mercies, that You prepare our hearts and make firm our thoughts, and make our prayers fluent in our mouths, and Your ears should hearken to the voice of Your servants' prayers, who pray unto You with the voice of supplication and broken spirit. And You, merciful G-d, with Your abundant mercies and great loving-kindness, shall forgive, pardon, and atone for us and for Your entire nation, the house of Israel, everything that we sinned, or have been perverse, or acted wantonly before You. Because it is open and known before You that it was not with rebelliousness or with defiance (Heaven forbid) that we disobeyed Your word and the words of the Torah and Your commandments, but because of the *yetzer* (evil inclination) that is constantly aflame within us, which does nor rest or cease until it brings us to the desires of this lowly world and its emptiness, and it confuses our thoughts, even when we stand in prayer before You to pray for our lives, it disturbs our thoughts with its manipulations, and we cannot withstand it because our minds have been so weakend, and bearing the burden of the many troubles, problems, and pressures has drained our energies.

Therefore, merciful and compassionate G-d, do with us as You promised Your trusted servant, "I shall show favor when I choose to show favor, and I shall show mercy when I choose to show mercy," and our Sages of blessed memory have said that this is even when one is not deserving and worthy, because that is Your way, to do good to both the good and the bad. For it is known and revealed before You our anguish and pain in that we are unable to bring ourselves closer to serve You and to devote our hearts to You, truthfully and totally. Alas for our souls, and woe unto us, our Father in Heaven.

May You arouse Your mercy and the great kindness You have for us, to banish and remove the evil inclination from within us, and rebuke it that it depart from us and not mislead us to deter us from Your service (Heaven forbid), and may no evil thought occur to us, neither while we are awake nor in a dream of the night, especially while we stand in prayer before You or when we learn Your Torah or when we perform Your mitzvos. May our minds be pure, lucid, clear, and truthfully firm and sincere as Your good will with us.

May You arouse our hearts and the hearts of Your entire nation Israel to proclaim Your Oneness in truth and with love, to serve You with a proper service that will be accepted before Your throne of glory, and fasten our belief in You that it be uninterrupted and bound in our hearts like a peg that will not slip. Heavenly Father, remove all the barriers that stand between us and You.

Save us from all obstacles and errors. Do not forsake us, abandon us or shame us. Be with our mouths when we speak, with our hands when we do, and with our hearts when we think. And may we merit, merciful G-d, that we restrict our hearts, thoughts, speech, and deeds, and all our movements and feelings, those that are known to us or unknown to us, those that are revealed or hidden, that all should be directed to You totally and in truth, without improper thought, Heaven forbid.

Purify our hearts and sanctify us. Pour pure water upon us and cleanse us, with Your love and Your compassion. Implant within our hearts love and reverence for You, constant, without interruption at all times and all places, as we walk, lie, and arise. May Your holy spirit burn within us, that our mainstay be in You, in Your greatness, Your awe, Your written and oral Torah, the revealed and the hidden, and in Your mitzvos, to proclaim the Oneness of Your mighty and awesome Name. Guard us from ulterior motives and vanity, from anger, irritability, sadness, talebearing, and other bad traits, and from anything that would impair Your holy and pure service which is so dear to us.

Make Your holy spirit flow upon us that we should cleave unto You and constantly increase our longing for You. Elevate us from level to level so that we merit reaching the level of our ancestors, Abraham, Isaac, and Jacob, and may their merit stand in our favor that You should hearken to the voice of our prayers, that we should always be responded to when we pray to You, whether for ourselves or for anyone of your nation Israel, for an individual or for a multitude.

May You rejoice and be proud of us, and may we produce fruits above and roots below. Do not remember for us our sins, especially the sins of our youth, as King David of blessed memory said, "Remember not the sins of my youth and my rebellion." Transform our sins and rebellion to merits, and make flow upon us from the world of *teshuvah* a constant thought to return unto You with sincerity, that we may rectify the defects we caused in Your holy and pure Names.

Guard us against envying one another, so that we should not envy anyone else and others should not envy us. To the contrary, put in our hearts that we should each see the virtues of our fellow people and not their faults, that we should each speak to our fellow in a way that is proper and desirable to You, and that no one should carry any enmity toward one's fellow.

Strengthen our bond in love for You, as it is known and revealed before You, that it all be pleasing to You, and that is our main intent. If we lack the wisdom to direct our hearts to You, then You teach us that we should know in truth the intention of Your good will. And with all this we plead before You, merciful G-d, that You accept our prayers with compassion and will. Amen. So may it be Your will.

How demanding Rebbe Elimelech was of himself can be seen from the following episode.

⌒ One day the *Chozeh* found Rebbe Elimelech profoundly distressed. Upon inquiry regarding the cause of his sadness, Rebbe Elimelech said, "How can I not be sad, having committed a sin?"

"What sin did the Rebbe commit?" the *Chozeh* asked.

Rebbe Elimelech said, "I was *davening Hodu*, and a woman came in crying desperately for help for her daughter, who was in difficult labor. I asked her for her name and her daughter's name, and that was an interruption in *davening*."

"But," the *Chozeh* said, "it is permitted to interrupt during *Hodu*, because it is before *Baruch She'amar.*"

"Yes," Rebbe Elimelech said, "in our *nusach Sefard* it is permissible. But inasmuch as in *nusach Ashkenaz Hodu* is after *Baruch She'amar,* I should not have interrupted during *Hodu.*"

Rebbe Elimelech said, "When people complain to me that they have no *parnassah* or ask for a *refuah* from illness, I know that I am at fault. If my *avodas Hashem* [service of Hashem] would be what it should be, these troubles would not have happened to them."

☞ On one occasion, when Rebbe Elimelech was sleeping, a person came with a desperate plea, and asked Rebbe Zusia to wake him. Rebbe Zusia put his hand over the *mezuzah*, and Rebbe Elimelech awoke.

Rebbe Zusia explained, "The Psalmist says, 'I have set Hashem before me always' [*Psalms* 16:8]. A person must always have the Name of Hashem before one's eyes. But how can one do this when one is asleep? One must rely on the Name of Hashem in the *mezuzah*. When I covered the *mezuzah*, Rebbe Elimelech awoke."

☞ Toward the end of his life, Rebbe Elimelech took hardly any nourishment. When his son Elazar pleaded with him to eat, he said, "If I could have the soup made by Chanala, the wife of the water-carrier, I would eat it."

The water-carrier was one of the hidden *tzaddikim* with whom Rebbe Elimelech occasionally met to study the secrets of Torah. Once, when he visited the water-carrier, Chanala wished to serve something to her honored guest, but there was no food in the kitchen. Chanala put up a pot of water and said, "*Ribono shel Olam* [Master of the Universe]! I have nothing to offer the great *tzaddik*. But you, *Ribono shel Olam*, have everything. You have *Gan Eden*. Please put some of the taste of *Gan Eden* into this pot."

The flavor of *Gan Eden* was the only nourishment Rebbe Elimelech desired.

Commentaries on Chassidic philosophy credit Rebbe Elimelech with making the affiliation with a *tzaddik* the center point of Chassidus. Indeed, the *sefer Noam Elimelech* is replete with the role of the *tzaddik* and the importance of achieving closeness to a *tzaddik*. But this concept is hardly original with Rebbe Elimelech. The Midrash comments on the verse (*Exodus* 14:31), "And they had faith in Hashem and in Moses, His servant": "If they had faith in Moses, they certainly had faith in Hashem. But, *this is to teach you that if one has faith in a shepherd [leader] of Israel, it is as though he had faith in the One Who uttered and created the world.*"

Similarly, "The Torah says, 'The people spoke against Hashem and Moses' (*Numbers* 21:5). If they could speak against Hashem, they could certainly speak against Moses. But this teaches that anyone who speaks against a shepherd of Israel is as though he spoke against the One Who uttered and created the world" (*Mechilta*). Two thousand years before Rebbe Elimelech, the Midrash drew an analogy between one's relationship to a *tzaddik* and one's relationship to Hashem.

☞ The *tzaddik,* Rebbe Aharon Leib (father of the great Rebbe Meir of Premishlan), was a follower of Rebbe Elimelech and came to spend Shabbos with him, and when Rebbe Elimelech saw him, he said, "Woe! Such *gaavah* [vanity, arrogance]."

Rebbe Aharon Leib returned to his quarters and did a thorough soul-searching, but was unable to discover in what way he was a *baal gaavah*. Shabbos morning, Rebbe Elimelech again greeted him with, "Woe! Such *gaavah*," and again Rebbe Aharon Leib's soul-searching turned up nothing. This scene repeated itself at *shalosh seudos* (the third Shabbos meal).

After Shabbos was over, Rebbe Aharon Leib asked, "In what way does the Rebbe see that I am a *baal gaavah*?"

Rebbe Elimelech said, "*Eliyahu HaNavi* [Elijah the prophet] complained to me that he has offered to teach you Torah, but you refused his offer. Isn't it *gaavah* to reject *Eliyahu HaNavi*?"

Rebbe Aharon Leib said, "Oh, so that's all it is! Well, I do not wish Torah to be *given* to me, and I will send him away again. Whatever I acquire of Torah must be by my own effort."

If this was a disciple of Rebbe Elimelech, imagine what the master was like!

It is related that when the *Chozeh* first set up court in Lanzhut, Rebbe Elimelech was upset. It must be understood that this was certainly not petty jealousy. After all, the Talmud says that a father is never envious of a son's success, and a teacher is not envious if a student excels more than he. Rebbe Elimelech's unhappiness can be understood from the following story.

☙ The Baal Shem Tov would *daven* the *Amidah* for an extraordinarily long time. His disciples, who concluded much earlier, would study Torah while waiting for the Baal Shem Tov to finish. On one such occasion, several of the disciples were hungry, and they knew they had ample time to leave the *beis midrash*, eat, and return before the Baal Shem Tov would finish *davening* the *Amidah*. To their surpise, when they returned, they found that the Baal Shem Tov had already concluded the *Amidah*.

The Baal Shem Tov explained, "A man wanted to reach something that was very high, but had no ladder. He had a person stand on someone's shoulders, and then climbed up and stood on that person's shoulders. If the first person moved away, the top person would not be able to reach the desired object.

"So it is with me," the Baal Shem Tov said to his disciples. "When you are all here, I can stand on your shoulders and reach very high levels in the celestial world. When you left, I had nothing to stand on, and I was unable to reach those levels, so I finished the *Amidah* more quickly."

When the *Chozeh* left Lizhensk to set up hs own court, Rebbe Elimelech felt that his ability to reach the highest celestial levels had been compromised.

☞ As was the case with many *tzaddikim*, Rebbe Elimelech could not sleep if any money remained in the house, feeling that it signified a lack of faith in Hashem's constant support. When his family saw him searching the house at night as if it were the search for the *chametz* before *Pesach*, they would join him. If no money could be found, he would send someone to the local inn to inquire if a traveler had lodged there prior to coming to see him, as sometimes people would entrust them with money to give to him. According to halachah, if someone had accepted money for him, that money immediately became his, and Rebbe Elimelech could not sleep if any money was in his possession.

That is exactly what happened one night. One of his chassidim, Reb Leibish, had come to Lizhensk, bringing *kvitlach* (petitions) and donations. Rebbe Elimelech could not sleep, and when the house search did not turn up any money, one of the Rebbe's children went to the inn. There he found Reb Leibish, who promptly came to the Rebbe and gave him the money. The Rebbe took the money and had it sent to the homes of the needy, slipped under the door so that they should not know that it had come from him.

The Rebbe asked, "The coachman who brought you to Lizhensk, where is he? Tell him to come here promptly."

What would the Rebbe want with this uncouth person? Reb Leibish wondered, *and how can I wake him up and tell him to go to the Rebbe? He might kill me for disturbing him.*

But the Rebbe's order was not to be defied. Reb Leibish had a difficult time rousing the coachman from a sound sleep. "Why are you waking me?" the coachman said.

"The Rebbe wants to see you at once," Reb Leibish said.

"Have you gone mad?" the coachman thundered. "You wake me up from a deep sleep and expect me to go to your Rebbe on a freezing night?" He picked up a chair with which to hit Reb Leibish, who managed to dodge the blow.

The coachman went back to bed and tossed and turned. *What does the Rebbe want of me?* he said to himself. He cursed Reb Leibish, but ultimately, when he could not fall asleep again, he said,

"I'll go to the Rebbe. Show me where he lives."

When the coachman entered the Rebbe's house, the Rebbe spoke harshly, "You evil sinner! Do you think that the world is a free-for-all, that one can do anything one wishes?"

The coachman was stunned. "What are you talking about? What kind of sins have I done? What do you want of me?"

Rebbe Elimelech said, "So, you want a list of your sins?" and he began enumerating all the sins the coachman had done. The coachman began to weep, and then fainted.

Rebbe Elimelech revived him. "Fainting will accomplish nothing," he said. "*Teshuvah!* Only *teshuvah* can help."

The coachman wept. "But there is no *teshuvah* for me. I have been leading a sinful life for years. I didn't even think that what I was doing was sinful."

"There is always *teshuvah*," Rebbe Elimelech said. "Stay in the *beis midrash* all day, *daven*, recite *Tehillim*, and beseech others to teach you the *Chumash*. If someone invites you for a meal, you may go, and if someone gives you food, you may eat. But you are not to ask anyone for food.

"Continue this for three years; then come back to me."

Three years later, the coachman returned. He had begun to study Torah, and had refined his ways.

Rebbe Elimelech embraced him, "Blessed is Hashem, Who desires *teshuvah,* and Who can lift a fallen person to the greatest spiritual heights."

The coachman moved his family to Lizhensk and remained a devoted follower of Rebbe Elimelech.

From *Emunei Am Segulah,* Rabbi Mordechai Gerlitz

One cannot write about Rebbe Reb Elimelech without mentioning his brother, Rebbe Reb Zusia. The two brothers went into self-imposed exile together.

My father used to relate the following story.

☞ During their wanderings, Rebbe Elimelech and Rebbe Zusia stopped off at an inn. Since no rooms were available, they slept on benches in the dining area. When the peasants came in and drank to intoxication, they began to dance in a circle. Whenever one particular peasant passed the bench on which Rebbe Zusia was sleeping, he delivered a hard blow, awakening the sleeper.

After several turns of the circle, Rebbe Elimelech said, "Brother, why should you be getting all the *petsch* [blows]? I deserve some *petsch*, too." Rebbe Zusia consented, and they traded places.

Upon the next turn of the dancers, just as the peasant was about to deliver a blow, his buddy said to him, "Why do you always hit the Jew on this bench? Why don't you hit the Jew on the next bench?" The buddy complied, again hitting Rebbe Zusia, who was now on the other bench.

Rebbe Zusia said, "If it is *bashert* [destined] that Zusia should get *petsch*, then Zusia will get *petsch*."

> *The concept of bashert is unclear. We are told that the income a person will earn each year is decreed on Rosh Hashanah. Why, then, do we all exert ourselves for parnassah (livelihood)? The issue of bitachon (trust) versus hishtadlus (effort) is discussed in many sifrei mussar, and the mussar authorities provide guidelines.*

Let me share with you this story, the Rav in the story being either R' Yeshaye Horowitz (*Shelah*) or R' Moshe Alschich.

> One Shabbos, the Rav delivered a *derashah* (sermon) in which he stated that a person's earnings are decreed on Rosh Hashanah, and a person cannot exceed this allotment by making extra effort, nor will less effort cause him to have less.

The Rav's sister was married to a simple but very pious Jew, a porter with a horse and wagon. On Sunday morning, he *davened* slowly and after breakfast sat down to say *Tehillim*. His wife asked why he wasn't going to work.

The husband said, "I don't have to. The Rav said that whatever Hashem decreed for me will come to me. I can learn *mishnayos* and say *Tehillim*."

The wife said, "That's not what the Rav meant."

"It is exactly what he meant," the husband said. "If you don't believe it, ask him yourself."

The wife went to the Rav and said, "My dear brother, you must be more careful what you say in your *derashos*. My husband took you seriously, and won't go to work."

The Rav said, "If he is sincere in his trust in Hashem, his *parnassah* will indeed come to him."

One day, a man came to the door. He saw a horse and wagon standing there, and wanted to know whether it was for rent. This man happened to be a highway robber, who had buried his loot. He rented the horse, and dug up his money. When he went down into the pit to see if he had left any coins behind, the walls collapsed and buried him. After standing there for several hours, the horse found its way home by habit, and the Rav's brother-in-law was enriched.

The Rav told his sister, "This happened because his trust in Hashem was simple and complete. Anything less than perfect trust would not have been effective."

☞ Rebbe Zusia once said to Rebbe Elimelech, "Brother, the *sefarim* say that the *neshamah* of *Adam HaRishon* contained the *neshamos* of all the human beings who would come into the world. That means that your *neshamah* and my *neshamah* were in Adam. How could you and I allow him to sin and eat from the Tree of Knowledge?"

Rebbe Elimelech answered, "Not only did I not stop Adam from eating the fruit, I actually encouraged him. You see, the serpent had lied, saying that G-d forbade eating the fruit of the Tree of Knowledge 'because G-d knows that on the day you eat of it, your eyes will be opened and you will be like G-d' [*Genesis* 3:5]. If Adam had not eaten from the fruit, he would have harbored the thought, 'Had I eaten from that tree, I could have been equal to G-d,' and he would have lived the rest of his life with that heresy. I decided it was better that he should eat from the tree and realize that no human being can be like G-d."

☞ One of Rebbe Elimelech's disciples asked for an explanation of the *kapparos* ritual. (A long-established practice during the Days of Penitence is that one takes a white chicken [a rooster for a male and a hen for a female] and recites the prayer for atonement. The chicken is then given to the poor.) Rebbe Elimelech directed the disciple to an inn to observe the innkeeper performing the ritual.

Upon observing the innkeeper fulfilling the custom, the disciple saw that he was a simple person, engaged all day in conversation with the peasants to whom he sold beer. What could the disciple possibly learn from such a man? However, he remained at the inn until the day before Yom Kippur.

On that day, he saw the innkeeper open a ledger and read aloud all the sins that he had committed during the year, with sighs of regret. When he finished this litany, he opened another ledger and read aloud the bad things that had happened to him during the year: A barrel of wine had soured, and that was a huge loss. His cow had died. A fire had destroyed one of the rooms in his inn. He had fallen and broken a leg. His wife had miscarried. One of his children had been seriously ill. His well had dried up.

After reading off this list, he put both ledgers together and said, "*Ribono shel Olam* [Master of the Universe], I know that I did many wrong things during the year, but You, *Ribono shel Olam*, decreed that many bad things should happen to me. Because tonight is Yom Kippur, let us both have a clean slate. Let us make an even exchange. I will forgive You, and You will forgive me."

When the disciple reported this to Rebbe Elimelech, the Rebbe said, "The great merit of this simple person is that he knows that everything happens only because Hashem wills it to happen. There are no spontaneous happenings. If bad things happened to him, they were not simply natural accidents;

rather, he attributed them to Hashem. This sincere, simple faith in Hashem warranted his being forgiven."

☞ From Rosh Chodesh Elul onward, Rebbe Elimelech was secluded in his study, and told his *gabbai* (attendant) that he was not to be disturbed except for a matter of the utmost urgency.

In a town some distance from Lizhensk lived a wealthy man whose son, a bright boy, suddenly became insane, talking irrationally and breaking objects. Doctors could do nothing for him, and the distraught father hired someone to watch the child. When the wealthy man heard that many people recovered from their illnesses following a *berachah* from Rebbe Elimelech, he decided he would take his son to the *tzaddik* for a *berachah*.

As they came closer to Lizhensk, they saw a poor person walking along the road. The boy said, "Father, give that poor man *tzeddakah*." The father was surprised to hear the boy say something rational, and he gave the man some money.

"Where are you going?" the man asked.

"To Lizhensk to get a *berachah* for my son from the *tzaddik*," the father said.

"There is no need for you to disturb Rebbe Elimelech," the man said. "You can see that your son is already well. Just your intention to go to the *tzaddik* merited his cure."

The father said, "You may be right, but having come all this way, I want to get a *berachah* from the *tzaddik*."

Arriving in Lizhensk, he prepared a *kvitel*, but when he tried to see Rebbe Elimelech, the *gabbai* said that the Rebbe could not be disturbed. The father pleaded with the *gabbai*, saying that he had come from such a long distance and that he would not take more than a moment's time.

The *gabbai* allowed the pair to go into Rebbe Elimelech. The father gave the Rebbe the *kvitel* and a large sum of money.

Rebbe Elimelech said, "Ay, Ay! To Elimelech you give so much more money than you gave to *Eliyahu HaNavi*!" Rebbe Elimelech blessed him and sent him on his way.

☞ One Rosh Chodesh Elul, Rebbe Elimelech appeared dejected. "The days of awe are approaching, and I have been so sinful. How will I come before Hashem, not having begun to do *teshuvah*?"

After a while he said, "Well, I will come before Hashem with my broken heart. 'Hashem is close to the brokenhearted'" (*Psalms* 34:19).

Teachings

King Solomon says, "A man has joy in the utterances of his mouth" (*Proverbs* 15:23). The word for "utterances" (*maaneh*) can also mean "poor" or "restricted." The verse is thus saying, "One who restricts his speech can have joy."

The prophet says, "'Can a person conceal himself in a secret place so that I shall not see him?' says Hashem" (*Jeremiah* 23:24). The Hebrew text also lends itself to be read, "If a person separates himself from the world and secludes himself to meditate, but thinks '*va'ani* — and I — am someone special,' then Hashem says, 'I shall not look at him'" (i.e., a person who acts like a *tzaddik*, but is vain and has an inflated ego, is not looked upon favorably by Hashem).

A man asked Rebbe Elimelech for a *berachah* because his memory was failing. Rebbe Elimelech said, "Do proper *teshuvah*, because the Talmud says that *teshuvah* is so great that it reaches the Throne of Glory [*Yoma* 86b], and in the Rosh Hashanah prayers we say, 'There is no forgetting before Your Throne of Glory.' If you reach the Throne of Glory with *teshuvah* you will not be forgetful."

The Torah says, "Yisro, the minister of Midian, the father-in-law of Moses, heard everything that Hashem did to Moses and to Israel" (*Exodus* 18:1). Why does it single out Moses? After all, Moses is included in "Israel."

The Torah is telling us that there were two redemptions. The Jews' primary redemption was from their enslavement and torture. Their redemption was a physical one. Moses, on the other hand, felt it was primarily a spiritual redemption, a separation from the pagan culture of Egypt to a spiritual life, which they acquired at Sinai. Therefore, Moses saw the redemption differently than the rest of Israel.

> *In the Haggadah From Bondage to Freedom, I pointed out that Pesach is not just an "Independence Day" celebration. No one celebrates Independence Day for an entire week. Furthermore, many times during the week we refer to the Exodus from Egypt, which is a central theme in Judaism.*
>
> *The Exodus should be understood to be more than liberation from the tyranny of Pharaoh. A person can be a slave to many*

> *things: One can be a slave to alcohol, to drugs, to food, to acclaim, to smoking, to making money, etc. Any habit from which one cannot readily break free is a kind of enslavement. The Torah wants us to be free to choose, and not be under any compulsion.*
>
> *The Exodus should therefore be seen primarily as a spiritual redemption.*

Hashem said to Abraham, "*Lech lecha,* Go into yourself" (*Genesis* 12:1). This means that one should look into oneself, to discover the character defects that are innate within a person, to eliminate one's bad *middos* (traits) and strengthen one's good *middos,* because only then can one appreciate the greatness of Hashem.

Hashem said to Abraham, "Gaze now toward the heavens and count the stars" (*Genesis* 15:5). That is, "Do not lower yourself from your spiritual status to indulge in earthly things. Rather, look up to the sky." A person can come to an understanding of the greatness of Hashem by studying the movement of the heavenly bodies.

> *Rambam says that the way a person can achieve love of Hashem and reverence for Hashem is by looking at the greatness of His creations (Yesodei HaTorah 2:2). This idea is expressed in Psalms 19:2, "The heavens declare the glory of Hashem," and in Isaiah 40:26, "Raise your eyes on high and see Who created these." The universe is the greatest testimony to the greatness of Hashem, but one must be willing to see it.*

The Torah says, "Hashem spoke all these statements, saying, 'I am Hashem, your G-d'" (*Exodus* 20:1). Rebbe Elimelech said, "All these statements' means everything in the Torah. The purpose of all the mitzvos in the Torah is to help us to know that Hashem is G-d."

> *The Talmud said that Moses taught us 613 mitzvos. King David said that they are all subsumed under eleven principles. Isaiah said they are contained within six principles, Michah said, within three, and the prophet Habakkuk said, within one principle: "The righteous person will live with his emunah" [Makkos 24a]. The goal of the entire Torah is to lead us to believe in Hashem, and if one truly believes in Hashem, one can easily come to all 613 mitzvos.*

"Hashem said to Moses and Aaron, saying: 'When Pharaoh speaks to you, saying, "Provide a wonder for yourselves" (*Exodus* 7:8). Rebbe Elimelech asks, "Why would Pharaoh say, 'Provide a wonder for *yourselves*'? If he wanted to test Moses' authenticity, he should have said, 'Show *me* a wonder.'"

Rebbe Elimelech said that a magician who uses sleight of hand knows exactly what the outcome of the trick will be. It appears to be magic only to the observer. However, if one invokes a Higher Power to perform a miracle, the invoker does not know exactly what miracle will appear. That is why Pharaoh would say, "Perform a miracle that is not sleight of hand, but is wondrous even to *you*."

Someone asked Rebbe Elimelech, "Why is there a need to consult a *tzaddik*? One can get all the guidance and teaching one needs from *sifrei mussar*."

Rebbe Elimelech answered, "The Torah says that Yisro came to the desert to Moses because he had heard of the great wonders Hashem had done for Israel [*Exodus* 18:1]. Rashi explains that he heard about the dividing of the Sea of Reeds and the battle of Amalek. What was it about the battle of Amalek that made Yisro come?

"Hearing about all the great wonders that Hashem wrought for Israel should have been enough reason for Yisro to believe in Hashem. But Amalek, too, had heard about the great wonders, as it says, 'Nations heard and they trembled' [*Exodus* 15:14], yet this did not deter Amalek from attacking Israel. Yisro reasoned, if even after hearing such great miracles one can deny Hashem, then one must attach himself to a *tzaddik* in order to believe in Hashem. That is why Yisro came to Moses."

> *Amalek is representative of the yetzer hara. Even after one studies the great works of mussar, the yetzer hara can incite a person to sin. The only way to resist the yetzer hara is to be close to a tzaddik, who can help a person resist the yetzer hara.*
>
> *Rebbe Simchah Bunim of Pshische had been a merchant associated with several other merchants at the market. He tried to impress upon them the importance of relating personally to a tzaddik. They saw no need for that, believing that one can obtain all the necessary guidance by reading sefarim.*
>
> *One day, they were on their way to the theater and invited Rebbe Simchah Bunim to join them, but he refused. When they returned, they were ecstatic. "You should have been there," they said to him.*
>
> *Rebbe Simchah Bunim said, "Why should I? I can read it."*
>
> *The theatergoers answered, "Reading the play doesn't compare to seeing it."*
>
> *Rebbe Simchah Bunim said, "That is precisely the point that I was making regarding a tzaddik."*

"(Yitzchak said,) 'See, now, I have aged; I know not the day of my death'" (*Genesis* 27:2). Rebbe Elimelech said, "When a person reaches old age, he may forget that he is mortal and may think that he is going to live forever."

Rebbe Elimelech said, "The *yetzer hara* told me, 'I'm warning you. Elimelech: Stop teaching *mussar* and guiding people to do what is right, because if you influence everyone to do good, what will become of me? No one will have any need for me, and I will be of no use. If you continue to preach *tzeddakah* and good deeds, I want you to know that I will concentrate all my forces against you, and you will not be able to resist me.'

"I answered the *yetzer hara,* 'I will not heed you in any way. Regardless of what I do, you will try to divert me from what is good and seduce me to sin. You show no favoritism to anyone. I will continue to do whatever I can to rescue people from your cunning.'"

Rabbi Elimelech said, "When Mashiach comes, those people who pursued material wealth will be taken to great treasuries where there are heaps of gold, silver, and jewels, and they will fill their pockets with this wealth.

"When Mashiach flies upward to *Gan Eden*, the *tzaddikim* will follow. Those who filled their pockets with gold, silver, and jewels will look up. Seeing the bliss of *Gan Eden*, they will desire to get there, but because they will be weighed down with all the wealth they stuffed into their pockets, they will be unable to lift themselves."

In the eternal world we will be rewarded with what we valued in life. A coachman will be given a fine coach and a team of horses, and

> *will drive infinitely, to his heart's content. Tzaddikim will bask in the glory of the Shechinah (Divine presence).*
>
> *Rebbe Moshe Teitelbaum (author of Yismach Moshe) dreamt that he was in Gan Eden, and saw the tzaddikim studying Torah. He thought, "Is this all there is to Gan Eden?"*
>
> *A heavenly voice proclaimed, "Moshe, son of Chanah! Do you think that the tzaddikim are in Gan Eden? Not so! Rather, Gan Eden is in the tzaddikim."*
>
> *This is also true of this world. People looking for happiness seek a place where they will be happy. However, true happiness is not external. True happiness is within a person. One need only look for it to find it.*

"Hashem spoke to Moses in the desert of Sinai, in the *Ohel Moed* [Tent of Meeting]" (*Numbers* 1:1). The Torah was given on Sinai, the lowest of the mountains, to impress upon us the importance of humility. On the verse, "From the desert, a gift" (ibid. 21:19), the Talmud says, "Anyone who makes himself *hefker* as the desert (i.e., open to everyone) will receive the Torah as a gift" (*Nedarim* 52b).

However, one must be cautious that humility, feeling oneself to be small, should not develop into *atzvus* (depression). *Avodas Hashem* requires that one be in a state of *simchah*.

Moed can mean *yom tov* (holiday), a day of *simchah*. The verse, "Hashem spoke to Moses in the desert of Sinai, in the *Ohel Moed*," can be understood to mean, "as humble as the Sinai desert, but joyful as a *moed*."

> *This theme is developed in Tanya. The Alter Rebbe points out that awareness of one's shortcomings may be necessary for humility, but*

> *this should not lead to atzvus. A person may be momentarily sad when reflecting on his shortcomings, but should quickly put this behind him and feel the joy of being privileged to serve Hashem.*

How can a person who has committed a sin with his hands do a mitzvah with the hands that have been tainted with sin?

One can do so by feeling oneself to be part of *Klal Yisrael*. The prophet says, "Your people are all righteous" (*Isaiah* 60:21). *Klal Yisrael*, taken as a whole, are all *tzaddikim*. When a person is bound to *Klal Yisrael*, that person is holy and without defect.

"Open for me the gates of righteousness, I will enter them and thank Hashem. This is the gate of Hashem" (*Psalms* 118:19-20). A *tzaddik* always feels that he has not done enough. He feels he is standing outside the gates of *avodas Hashem*, not yet having entered. The Psalmist says, "This feeling of humility is indeed the gate to Hashem."

Stories

In a village near Lizhensk lived a young man, Bentzi, whose parents had both died when he was a child. The people of the community looked after his needs and cared for him. When he was a bit older, a wealthy member of the community gave him a job in his business. Bentzi gave his earnings to his employer for safekeeping.

Bentzi began thinking about his future. He was an orphan; who would help him find a *shidduch*? Whenever his employer sent him to Lizhensk, he would ask Rebbe Elimelech what to do.

Rebbe Elimelech said to him, "A young woman, Bluma, is employed in my home. She is a very fine person and deserves more than I can pay her. Perhaps your employer can find a job for her."

Bentzi carried the message, and indeed, Bluma went to work for Bentzi's employer. Rebbe Elimelech said to Bentzi, "Bluma is an orphan. Keep an eye on her and help her in any way you can."

Bentzi told Bluma about her new position, saying that the employer was an honest and caring person to whom he entrusted his earnings for safekeeping. Bluma said she would do likewise.

The employer often thought that Bentzi and Bluma were a perfect match, but, since the two knew each other, he did not feel that he should initiate a *shidduch*. Bentzi, on the other hand, hesitated to ask his employer to act as a matchmaker. In another year he would have saved enough money to go into business and support a family, and then, he thought, he would talk to Bluma about marriage.

One night, a fire broke out and destroyed the employer's business. He was left destitute, as were Bentzi and Bluma. They went to other villages to find work, and Bluma found a job that would pay her 50 gulden a year. Bentzi could have found a better-paying job elsewhere, but Rebbe Elimelech had assigned him to look after Bluma, so he took a job nearby for 50 gulden a year. At the end of the year, Bentzi suggested to Bluma that they pool their savings and buy a horse and wagon. They could cut firewood in the forest and sell it in town. "We can be partners in the business," he said.

One day, a group of beggars came to town, and Bentzi was horrified to see his former employer among them, clad in tattered clothes. Bentzi asked him, "Isn't there anything you can do for yourself to earn a respectable living?"

The employer said, "Yes, I think I could start a business if I had 100 gulden, but I am penniless. I live from hand to mouth."

Bentzi rushed to Bluma and told her about their former employer's plight. "He was always so kind to us. I am willing to give him my 50 gulden. Would you give him yours? We are still young and we can help ourselves, but if he doesn't have the means to help himself, he will be doomed to be a beggar for the rest of his life."

Bluma did not hesitate. She handed Bentzi the 50 gulden and broke down in tears. "Now I am destitute again, with no one to care for me. I had hoped that one day, maybe you and I …."

"What are you saying, Bluma?" Bentzi asked. "I was always interested in you, but did not have the nerve to ask you. Perhaps our doing this mitzvah is Hashem's way of bringing us together. Mazal tov!"

Bluma responded, "Mazal tov, Bentzi, but hurry with the money before our employer leaves town with the troop of beggars."

Bentzi gave the man the money, and the grateful former employer blessed him.

Bluma found a job as a domestic, and Bentzi, without a horse and wagon, cut firewood and brought it into town, eventually saving up enough money to be married. Bluma said, "Before we are married we must go to Lizhensk to ask for the Rebbe's *berachah*."

Rebbe Elimelech arranged a wedding for the couple, and his joy was exuberant. He said, "It is customary to announce the wedding gifts. I give the couple the nearby village."

Rebbe Naftali of Ropschitz, a disciple of Rebbe Elimelech, said, "And I give them the mill adjacent to the river."

Another disciple said, "I give them 1000 ducats," and another disciple added, "I, too, give them 1000 ducats."

The feast was concluded with the *sheva berachos*. Bentzi and Bluma left, and Bentzi said, "Let me show you where I cut wood in the forest."

As they walked through the woods, they heard a cry for help, and found a man struggling in quicksand. Bentzi tore his jacket into strips to fashion a makeshift rope, and he and Bluma pulled the man out. He said that he was the son of the *poritz* (feudal lord), and his marriage had taken place that night. He had gone out to the woods to walk off his drunkenness and fell into the quicksand.

Bentzi and Bluma escorted the young man to the castle, where his distraught parents were agonizing over his absence. The young man told his parents how this young couple had saved his life.

The grateful *poritz* said, "As a reward for saving my son, I give you the nearby village as your own."

The bride's father, also a *poritz*, said, "And I give them the mill adjacent to the river."

The young man's mother said, "And I give them 1000 ducats." The bride's mother also gave 1000 ducats.

The Talmud says that when a *tzaddik* decrees, Hashem will fulfill his wish. Bentzi's and Bluma's selflessness, giving everything they owned to help their former employer, was a mitzvah that brought them great reward.

Bemeonos Arayos, Eliahu Ki Tov

As mentioned, volumes could be written about Rebbe Elimelech, but our purpose is to see how his four disciples used his bequests.

Rebbe Yisrael Haupstein
the Maggid of Kozhnitz (1737-1814)[1]

One Friday night, at the *seudas Shabbos*, the Baal Shem Tov's disciples noticed that he was smiling. After *havdalah* he traveled to Apta with a few disciples. There he sent for Shabsi, the bookbinder.

Shabsi was very anxious. What could the Baal Shem Tov want with a simple person like him? Ah, yes, he knew. The Baal Shem Tov was going to chastise him for his behavior on Friday night.

Indeed, when the Baal Shem Tov greeted him, he said, "Shabsi, what happened Friday night?"

Almost trembling, Shabsi said, "I had no money for Shabbos. No food, no challos, not even candles. I told my wife not to ask for help from anyone, and I was resigned to a bleak Shabbos. Then I left for the *beis midrash* to review the *parashah* and say *Tehillim* and *Shir HaShirim*.

"My wife is a true *tzaddekes* [pious woman], and not having anything to cook, she decided to clean the house thoroughly in honor of Shabbos. In doing so, she found in a crevice two pearls from the headpiece that she had worn as a bride. She took them into town, sold them, and bought all the necessary provisions for Shabbos.

"When I came home, I saw light shining from the window. I was confused, because I knew we had no candles. When I entered the

---

1. In this section, the term "Maggid" refers to the Maggid of Kozhnitz.

house and saw the table set for a feast, I concluded that my wife must have asked someone for money, and I was upset that she had gone against my wishes. My wife said that in cleaning the house for Shabbos, she had found the two pearls. I was overjoyed, knowing that this was a gift from Hashem to give me an *oneg Shabbos* pleasant Shabbos. I was so overcome with joy that, along with my wife, I began to dance. We danced around the table for almost an hour. I know this may not be proper, but I could not contain myself."

The Baal Shem Tov said, "Shabsi, when you danced around the table filled with the joy of Shabbos, the heavenly angels danced with you, and this caused great joy in the celestial spheres. You deserve a great reward for this. What is your wish?"

Shabsi said, "It is many years since our marriage, and we have no children."

The Baal Shem Tov said, "You will have a son this year, Shabsi, and you are to give him my name, Yisrael."

That year Shabsi's wife bore a son, whom they named Yisrael, and who became the great Maggid of Kozhnitz. Little wonder that he was often called "the second Baal Shem Tov."

Although the Maggid was born in 1737 and the Baal Shem Tov died in 1760, so that the Maggid was 23 when the Baal Shem Tov died, there is no record of the Maggid ever visiting the Baal Shem Tov. This is not too surprising. Many *tzaddikim* designated which students were to be their disciples and which were to follow other masters. For example, the Baal Shem Tov saw Rebbe Shneur Zalman (author of *Tanya*) as a child, but never again. He told his successor, Rebbe DovBer of Mezeritch, "He belongs to you, not to me."

The only communication the Maggid had with the Baal Shem Tov was in a dream, which the Maggid relates in *Avodas Yisrael*. He asked the Baal Shem Tov why, in his early exposure to *tzaddikim*, he had felt substantial progress in Torah study from day to day, whereas at that point there seemed to be hardly any growth day to day.

The Baal Shem Tov answered that when a child learns to read the *siddur* and the *Chumash*, there is a notable increase in what he learns daily or weekly. Once he becomes fluent in his studies, the changes from day to day are less dramatic.

Another story about the birth of the Maggid seems to contradict the first version. We have no way of knowing which is accurate, but since each has a lesson to be learned, I decided to include both.

☛ A woman came to the Maggid, complaining tearfully that she had been married for a number of years but had not had a child. "What are you willing to do about it?" the Maggid asked. The woman did not know what to say.

"My mother," the Maggid said, "was aging and still had no child. Then she heard that the Baal Shem Tov, who was traveling, was stopping briefly in Apta, so she hurried to him and asked for a *berachah* that she might have a child. 'What are you willing to do about it?' the Baal Shem Tov asked.

"My mother said, 'My husband is a poor bookbinder, but I do have one fine thing I can give the Rebbe.' She hurried home and fetched her good cape, which had been stored in a chest.

"When she returned to the inn where the Baal Shem Tov had lodged, she was told that he had already left for Medzhibozh. She immediately set out after him, but having no money to pay for a ride, she walked from town to town until she reached Medzhibozh. The Baal Shem Tov took the cape and hung it on the wall. 'It is well,' he said.

"My mother then walked all the way back, from town to town, until she reached Apta. A year later, I was born."

"Oh," the woman said, "I will bring you a beautiful cape of mine so that I may have a child."

The Maggid shook his head. "That won't work. You heard the story. My mother had no story to go by."

Tales of Hasidim

We find that after the sin of the Golden Calf, the Jews repented, and Moses was able to obtain forgiveness for them. However, after the sin of the spies, they also repented, but they were not forgiven (Numbers 14:39-45). Why?

Because at the sin of the Golden Calf, they were not aware that repentance can earn forgiveness, and their remorse was sincere. After the sin of the spies, they already knew that repentance can earn forgiveness; hence, they repented for an ulterior motive, and did not merit forgiveness.

Like many other *tzaddikim*, the Maggid was a Torah prodigy, learning much Talmud as a child. His father discouraged him from indulging in childish activities. At the age of 13, young Yisrael left home to increase his Torah knowledge by studying with the outstanding Torah scholars of the time.

The Maggid was widely respected as a preeminent Torah scholar. His Torah genius can be seen in his correspondence with Rebbe Pinchas Horowitz (author of *Haflaah*). No less a Torah giant than

Rebbe Chaim of Volozhin said to Rav Yaakov Meir Padwa of Brisk, "When I passed through Kozhnitz, I spent an entire day discussing Torah with the Rebbe of Kozhnitz, and I found him to be fluent in Talmud Bavli with the text of *Tosafos baal peh* [from memory], in addition to being *baki* [thoroughly knowledgeable] in the Jerusalem Talmud and in the earlier and later *poskim* [halachic authorities]."

☞ The Maggid held his father in high esteem. The Maggid's son, Rebbe Moshe Elyakim Bereiah, related that one Simchas Torah, the Maggid was unusually jubilant at the *hakafos*.

"I did not have the audacity to inquire what was so special about this Simchas Torah, but my brother-in-law did ask.

"The Maggid said, 'My father is in *Gan Eden* together with Reb Yochai, the father of Reb Shimon. Reb Yochai asked my father to take him along to my *hakafos*, and he would reciprocate by taking my father to Reb Shimon on Lag B'Omer. Joined by these two guests, is it any wonder that my *simchah* is so great?'"

☞ The Maggid returned to Apta annually for his father's *yahrzeit*, and was always asked to speak in the shul. He once said, "Why should I speak? Have you observed what I told you last year?"

One of the less-learned citizens said, "Does the Rebbe think he accomplished nothing with his *drashah* last year? I heard the Rebbe say that a Jew should always have Hashem's Name before him, and since then, I constantly see Hashem's Name before me, and it gives me *yiras Shamayim* [reverence for Hashem]."

The Maggid said, "If so, then I'll be glad to speak."

☞ The Maggid continued his Torah study under the tutelage of Rebbe Shmelke of Nikolsburg. A book dealer brought him the newly printed *sefer*, *Magen Avraham*, and the Maggid felt an exquisite holy light upon learning from it. He wanted to know what was so special about this *sefer*, and went to ask Rebbe Shmelke. Before he could utter a word, Rebbe Shmelke said, "Yisrael! You must have been learning *Magen Avraham*. The study of this *sefer* ignites great light within a person."

Through Rebbe Shmelke's influence, the Maggid visited Rebbe DovBer, the Maggid of Mezeritch, who said to Rebbe Shneur Zalman, "This young man will edit the *siddur* of the Arizal for us."

When the Maggid settled in Kozhnitz, Rebbe DovBer said, "Now they will say *Kesser* in Poland." This is a reference to *nusach Sefard*, in which the *Mussaf kedushah* on Shabbos begins with *Kesser*, whereas *nusach Ashkenaz*, which had prevailed in Poland, begins the *kedushah* with *Naaritzcha*.

The Maggid said, "I had studied 800 works on *kabbalah*, and when I came to Mezeritch I found that I had not even begun."

After the death of Rebbe DovBer, the Maggid became a devoted follower of Rebbe Elimelech of Lizhensk.

It was known that when Rebbe Elimelech accepted a disciple, the Rebbe would go out to greet him. When the Maggid came to Rebbe Elimelech, the Rebbe was asleep. The Maggid took this as a sign that he was not worthy, and returned to his lodging, brokenhearted. After a while, Rebbe Elimelech came to him and said, "An angel woke me and told me that I must hurry to greet you."

☞ There are countless stories of miraculous cures wrought by the Maggid. He was highly respected by the government officials. A duchess once approached him to bless her son, who had paralysis of both legs. The Maggid said, "Only if you promise me that you will not allow any anti-Semitic laws to be decreed." When she promised, the Maggid gave the boy his pipe and said, "Go fetch me fire to light my pipe." The boy promptly stood up and walked to the fireplace to bring a burning twig to the Maggid. The word of this miracle spread throughout the duchy.

The duke's brother did not believe this story and wanted to prove that the Maggid was a fraud. He went to the Maggid to ask for a blessing for his child who was seriously ill, and the Maggid said, "Hurry home! You may still find him alive."

The duke said, "See! He is a fraud. My son is perfectly healthy," and he did not hurry home. When he came home, he found that his son had fallen sick and died.

☞ The gaon, R' Yaakov Meshulam Ornstein, author of the responsa *Yeshuos Yaakov*, was consulted by a woman whose husband had disappeared. It was rumored that he had died. The *Yeshuos Yaakov* gathered evidence and wrote a long responsum, concluding that the husband can be assumed to have died, and that the wife may remarry. However, he requested that they obtain the Maggid of Kozhnitz' concurrence to his ruling.

The Maggid did not agree with the conclusion. He refuted the *Yeshuos Yaakov*'s analysis. The *Yeshuos Yaakov* defended his position, but the Maggid did not respond. The *Yeshuos Yaakov* then wrote asking why he had not responded.

The Maggid wrote back, "The interpretation of the *Tosafos* upon which you base your argument is erroneous, as you will see when the husband comes to you very much alive." Just as the *Yeshuos Yaakov* finished reading the letter, there was a tumult, because the husband was found to be alive and had been brought to him.

☞ Perhaps the greatest miracle is that, although the Maggid was very frail and so weak that he spent most of the day in bed, and was carried to the shul in his bed, as soon as they entered the shul, he jumped up and ran to the *amud* (pulpit), lit the menorah, and danced before the *amud*. He would *daven* in a loud voice that caused the windows to vibrate, and he could go on for hours. Then they would spread out a fur blanket for him to lie on until he was carried home.

☞ Rebbe Elimelech bequeathed to the Maggid the spirit of his heart, and indeed, the heart of the Maggid overflowed with love of Hashem, love of the Torah, and *ahavas Yisrael*.

☞ Rebbe Tzvi Elimelech (author of *Bnei Yisasschar*) was in Rimanov, and one Shabbos at *shalosh seudos* (the third Shabbos meal), Rebbe Menachem Mendel said, "Anyone in this generation who does not see the Maggid of Kozhnitz will not merit to greet Mashiach."

Immediately after *havdalah,* Rebbe Tzvi Elimelech departed for Kozhnitz. He feared that if he delayed, Mashiach might come and he would not be able to greet him. Not having money to pay for transportation, he trekked all the way to Kozhnitz.

When he arrived in Kozhnitz, he was told that the Maggid was resting in a room adjacent to the *beis midrash*. Entering the room, he saw that people had surrounded the Maggid's bed, and he was unable to see the Maggid, He managed to lift himself up so he could see over their heads, and when he saw the Maggid, the latter raised his head and quoted the Talmudic statement, "One can acquire something just by looking at it" (*Bava Metzia* 2a).

☞ Before the Shabbos on which the portion of the Torah containing the *Tochachah* (the dire warnings about what will befall Israel if they deviate from Torah observance) is read, the *Chozeh* told his chassidim to go to Kozhnitz, saying, "When the Maggid of Kozhnitz reads the *Tochachah*, one hears only *berachos*."

One disciple, Reb Mordechai, went to Kozhnitz to hear the curses transformed into blessings. When the Maggid read, "I will make your cities into ruins and I will destroy your Sanctuary and I will not accept the fragrance of your offerings," Reb Mordechai called out, "Heavenly Father! May we merit that wonderful time." He had heard only a blessing.

☞ A woman once came to the Maggid while he was reviewing the *parashah*. She waited patiently at the door. After a while, the Maggid looked up. "Your name is Leah bas Zissel?" he said.

The woman said, "Yes."

"And you've come for a *berachah* to have a child?"

The woman again responded, "Yes."

"Hashem will bless you with a child," the Maggid said. "I

just read in the Torah, וְטַפְּכֶם אֲשֶׁר אֲמַרְתֶּם לָבַז יִהְיֶה, [*Deuteronomy* 1:39], which means טַפְּכֶם, your children, אֲשֶׁר אֲמַרְתֶּם, that you said, לָבַז, for **לֵאָה בַּת זִיסְל**, **L**eah **B**as **Zissel**, it shall be.

☞ The Maggid once asked Rebbe Levi Yitzchak of Berditchev what time he *davened* in the morning. Rebbe Levi Yitzchak responded that it took a long time for him to prepare for *davening*, especially on Rosh Hashanah and Yom Kippur.

"And I *daven* early," the Maggid said.

"If so," Rebbe Levi Yitzchak said, "I will show you that I will nevertheless blow shofar before you."

On Rosh Hashanah, when preparing for sounding the shofar, the Maggid sensed that things were not going well for *Klal Yisrael*. Satan was bringing serious charges against them. The Maggid prayed fervently to counteract Satan, and, in a state of exhaustion, fell asleep.

The Maggid dreamed that he was in heaven and witnessed Satan's accusations. Suddenly, there was a loud tumult, which was caused by Rebbe Levi Yitzchak going to the *mikveh* in preparation for blowing the shofar.

When the Maggid awoke, he said, "It is apparent that we must wait for Rebbe Levi Yitzchak to blow shofar to subdue Satan. Only then will we be able to blow shofar."

☞ A chassid came to the Maggid, saying that he operated an inn in the countryside, and he wished to move to the city, where he would have the opportunity to *daven* with a *minyan*.

The Maggid said, "This is what you should do. If a wayfarer stops at your inn, greet him warmly, and offer him something to eat and drink, then prepare a place for him to sleep. Before he leaves, give him *tzeddakah* and escort him to the path.

"The Talmud says that *hachnassas orchim* [hospitality to wayfarers] is superior to greeting the *Shechinah* [*Shabbos* 127a]. If you will fulfill the mitzvah of *hachnassas orchim,* that is as important as *davening* with a *minyan.*"

The "spirit of the heart" that Rebbe Elimelech bequeathed to the Maggid can be seen in the following episode.

☞ On Yom Kippur eve, when the Maggid recited, "Hashem said, 'I have forgiven according to your words,'" he wept profusely, pleading for forgiveness for *Klal Yisrael.* "*Ribono shel Olam,*" he said. "If You think there are not enough *tzaddikim,* why, there is Rebbe Mendel of Rimanov, who is equal to all the *tzaddikim* of the generation. If You say that without the *Urim VeTumim* [the parchment contained in the High Priest's breastplate, wherewith Hashem responded to questions asked by the leader of Israel], there can be no forgiveness, why, in Lublin there is Rebbe Yaakov Yitzchak [the *Chozeh*], whose vision is as true as the *Urim VeTumim.* And if You say that there is no *Kohen Gadol,* why, Rebbe Levi Yitzchak of Berditchev performs the service no less than the *Kohen Gadol.* And if You say that Jews have not done adequate *teshuvah,* then I, with my frail body, accept on myself to do *teshuvah* for *Klal Yisrael. Ribono shel Olam,* is it so difficult for You to utter just the one word, *Salachti* [I have forgiven]?"

A moment later, he joyously exclaimed, "Hashem said, 'I have forgiven according to your words.'"

The Rebbe of Rhizin heard this and said, "I firmly believe that the Maggid heard Hashem say, '*Salachti*,' just as He said to Moses; otherwise, the Maggid would not have been joyous."

☞ On Erev Yom Kippur, people would come to the Maggid's door with their families, weeping over their sins and praying for a *chasimah tovah* (a favorable final judgment). The Maggid wept along with them, saying, "I am more sinful than you."

☞ At midnight, the Maggid said the prayers of lamentation for the loss of the *Beis HaMikdash*, and his tearful prayers would enter the Gates of Heaven, as the Talmud says, "The gates of tears are never closed" (*Berachos* 32b). He would enter pleas for the sick and needy, and his pleas were not refused, except once. He asked for an explanation, which was revealed to him.

That night, Rebbe Naftali of Ropshitz was on his way to Kozhnitz. A lively wedding party was taking place in the inn where he stopped to rest, and Rebbe Naftali could not help noticing that the bride appeared downcast. "Why are you sad?" he asked. "Everyone here seems to be celebrating."

"I'm sad because we have no *badchan* [jester]," she said.

"Is that all?" Rebbe Naftali said. "Then don't be sad. I was sent here *min haShamayim* by Heaven to dispel your sadness. I am a professional *badchan*, a wedding specialist."

With that, Rebbe Naftali stepped up onto a table, and began composing warm-hearted, witty rhymes about the *chasan* and *kallah,* the *mechutanim*, the guests, and even the innkeeper.

Soon everyone was laughing at his quips, but Rebbe Naftali's rhymes were not just humorous. Although the guests did not understand them, his rhymes contained esoteric messages, with many kabbalistic references. Not only was the wedding party entertained, but the Sages in Heaven interrupted their Torah study to listen to Rebbe Naftali, and the heavenly angels gathered to hear the unique praises of Hashem hidden in his words. The host of Heaven was so occupied in listening to Rebbe Naftali, and no one could convey the Maggid's midnight prayers.

After the wedding, Rebbe Naftali continued on to Kozhnitz. The Maggid greeted him. "Naftali, Naftali," he said. "What I cannot accomplish with tears, you accomplish with laughter."

Chassidic teachings place great emphasis on simchah. Rebbe Levi Yitzchak of Berditchev said that the most perilous moment for the Jews in the Purim story was when "That day, Haman went out joyful and exuberant" (Esther 5:9), because with simchah, even a rasha can wield great power. The turn of events in favor of the Jews was when "Haman hurried home, despondent and with his head covered (ibid., 6:12). That is why Rebbe Naftali's generating simchah at the wedding overrode the Maggid's tearful prayers.

Teachings

The Maggid quoted the mishnah, "Jealousy, lust, and glory remove a person from the world" (*Ethics of the Fathers* 4:28). "We can see this at the beginning of the Torah. Jealousy — Cain killed Abel (the Midrash states that he was envious of Abel). Lust — the generation of the Flood. Glory — the generation of the tower of Babel ('Let us make a name for ourselves' [*Genesis* 11:4])."

☞ A villager complained to the Maggid that he was careful to fulfill the mitzvah of *hachnassas orchim*. Why did the merit of this great mitzvah not protect him from losing his home in a fire?
The Maggid said, "The Torah says that the patriarch Abraham planted a tree in Beer Sheba. The word for tree is *eishel*, אֵשֶׁל, which stands for *achilah,* אֲכִילָה (eating), *shesiah,* שְׁתִיָּה (drinking), and *linah,* לִינָה (providing lodging). You provided people with food and drink, but not with lodging, so all you had was *eish*, אֵשׁ (fire), and that is why you suffered a fire."

The Maggid said, "In the *kedushah* of Shabbos *Mussaf*, we say that the angels declare, 'Where is the place of His glory?' Why do they ask that? The entire universe is full of the glory of Hashem."
The Maggid explained, "If a king visits a foreign country and is shown great honor there, that is indeed a glory for him. However, in his own country, it is taken for granted that he must be honored. That is why the angels say, if there was a place where Hashem were not present, there it would be great glory for Him to be honored, but inasmuch as Hashem is everywhere, it is all 'His country.' How, then, can we show Him special honor?"

In the Hoshana prayers we say that Israel shoulders Your burden. The Maggid said, "The word סִבְלָךְ has an additional meaning. The Talmud refers to the gifts that a *chasan* sends to his *kallah* as סִבְלוֹנוֹת "A *chasan* sent gifts to his *kallah*. She wrote to him, 'I have a fear that you may abandon me.'

"The *chasan* answered, 'Look at the gifts I sent you. As long as you have those gifts, you know that I want our relationship.'

"The Midrash compares the relationship of Hashem to Israel as that of a *chasan* to a *kallah*. The Torah is Hashem's gift to Israel (*Psalms* 68:19). As long as we have the Torah, we know that Hashem will not forsake us. Thus we say, הוֹשַׁעְנָא סוֹבֶלֶת סִבְלָךְ, Help those who have Your סִבְלוֹנוֹת gift, the Torah."

There is a disagreement between *Klal Yisrael* amd Hashem. Hashem says, "Return to Me, and I will return to you" (*Malachi* 3:7), requiring that *Klal Yisrael* take the initiative. *Klal Yisrael* says. "Bring us back to You, Hashem, and we shall return" (*Lamentations* 5:21), asking Hashem to take the initiative.

The Maggid cited the verse immediately preceding the verse in *Lamentations*, "Why do You ignore us eternally, forsake us for so long?" and commented that the word *lanetzach,* translated as "eternally," can also be translated as *nitzachon,* which means "triumph." The verse then reads, "Why do You ignore us *to triumph* over us, by winning the dispute as to who should take the initiative? It would be better if You let us triumph, as when the Sages overruled a heavenly voice, and You said, 'My children have triumphed over Me'" (*Bava Metzia* 59b). As Rebbe Elimelech said, "We say in our *tefillah*, הַנּוֹי וְהַנֵּצַח לְחַי עוֹלָמִים — the adornment and the triumph is to the Life-giver of the world.' Hashem considers it an adornment when His children triumph over him."

The Maggid said, "*Tzaddikim* who are totally devoted to Hashem are in a constant state of repentance and humility, and because they feel that they are distancing themselves from Hashem, they redouble their efforts to come closer to Him. Not so people who live in sin and falsehood, who deceive themselves that their ways are righteous and praise themselves that they serve Hashem."

"A person who does mitzvos in order to get reward is not serving Hashem. Rather, he is serving himself."

> *Serving oneself rather than serving Hashem is a form of idolatry. On the verse, "There shall be no foreign god within you" (Psalms 81:10), the Talmud comments, "What foreign god is within a person? The yetzer hara [evil inclination]" (Shabbos 105b). The Talmud sees a person who is interested only in satisfying his or her own desires as being essentially an idolater.*
>
> *Idolatry has little to do with statues. In the Scriptures we find the prophets reprimanding Jews for idolatry. How could it be that Jews, who had difficulty believing in Hashem despite witnessing countless miracles, would believe in an idol? The Talmud says that the Jews never believed there was any substance to the idols. They wanted to gratify the desires that Torah forbids, so they created an authority that would permit them to do so (Sanhedrin 63b). Idolatry is nothing but refusal of any restrictions on self-gratification.*

"When Hashem tests a person, He conceals His *kedushah* from him, because if he were aware of the imminent presence of Hashem, it would not be a test. One does not defy the king to his face. Therefore, every test includes a concealment of Hashem's presence."

> *The Baal Shem Tov said, "Once you know it is a concealment, it is no longer a concealment. The tragedy is that the concealment*

may be concealed: i.e., it does not occur to a person that there is a concealment.

In the prayer *Avinu Malkeinu*, we pray, אָבִינוּ מַלְכֵּנוּ הָרֵם קֶרֶן יִשְׂרָאֵל עַמֶּךָ — Our Father, Our King, raise high the pride of Israel, Your People. The word קֶרֶן, translated as "pride," has another meaning. If one invests money for a profitable return, the principal is referred to as קֶרֶן, and the profit is רֶוַח.

The Maggid cited the Talmud, "Hashem did not exile the Jews among the nations for any reason other than to attract converts" (*Pesachim* 87b). Thus, Hashem "invested" the Jews among the nations. The Maggid said that we pray, "Our Father, Our King, lift the קֶרֶן out of exile. The investment is not working, You are losing principal instead of making a profit."

Some people think that Hashem resides high in Heaven, and that they must elevate themselves in order to reach Him. They are wrong. The Midrash says that Hashem desired to have a presence in the lower world, and He makes His presence with the humble and lowly (*Isaiah* 57:15). Therefore, let a person humble himself, and he will come close to Hashem.

Hashem punished Cain for the murder of his brother, "You shall become a vagrant and a wanderer on earth" (*Genesis* 4:14), but couldn't Cain have decided to settle in one place?

Cain was punished with anxiety, so that he was never at peace, and he sought to escape the torture of anxiety by changing his location. The anxiety was the result of the guilt for his nefarious deed. His fears did not allow him to remain in one place.

> *This is psychologically true. An anxious person may seek a variety of "geographic" cures, trying to escape his anxiety by changing his environment. Had Cain done adequate teshuvah, he would have been relieved of his anxiety.*
>
> *In the Tochachah we read, "You will flee with no one pursuing you" (Leviticus 26:17). This does not mean that Hashem will inflict this punishment, but rather that their sins will cause them such severe anxiety that they will try to run from it. "Sinners are pursued by evil" (Proverbs 13:21).*
>
> *Some people try to run from themselves in a variety of ways: environmental changes, alcohol, drugs, gambling, seeking wealth or acclaim. None of these can alleviate anxiety, and like Cain, one remains forever a wanderer, wandering from one futile escape maneuver to another.*

The Talmud stresses the importance of *tefillah betzibbur* (communal prayer). The Maggid said, "If ten people gather together in shul to *daven*, and each prays for his own needs, that is not yet a unified *tzibbur*. If they all concentrate on the unity of Hashem, praying that His glory be revealed to the entire world, they are bonded into one unit."

There are *tzaddikim* who complete their holy mission in this world and, therefore, leave it. The secret to long life is to constantly be involved in a new mission.

> *This concept can be illustrated by the case of a person whose entire life was spent working. When he retires, he has nothing to do. Time weighs heavy on his hands and life may become unbearable.*

> *Spiritually, one can always find that there is something more that can be done. This is why the Psalmist says of the righteous, "They will be fruitful in old age, vigorous and fresh they will be" (Psalms 92:15). In the service of Hashem, one can always find something that needs to be done.*

R' Yochanan ben Zakkai said to his five disciples, "Go out and see which is the best way to which a person should adhere" (*Ethics of the Fathers* 2:13). What is meant by the expression, "Go out and see"? Where were they supposed to go?

The Maggid said that R' Yochanan ben Zakkai had many students, as is evident from the Talmud, which states that he lectured in the shade of the *Beis HaMikdash*, the only place where there was enough shade to accommodate all his students (*Pesachim* 26a). These five disciples were his prize students, of extremely high spirituality, who were totally devoted to Hashem and had no contact with worldly things. R' Yochanan told them that because they are totally occupied with *avodas Hashem*, they are unaware of the needs of ordinary people, whose everyday lives are in the material world.

In order for them to teach the common folk the proper way of life, they must temporarily descend from their high spiritual level, to appreciate the needs of people who are not at such a high level of spirituality. This is what R' Yochanan meant by, "Go out and see" — Leave your high level of spirituality temporarily.

> *This may explain why Moses was not permitted to bring the Israelites into Eretz Yisrael. The Torah relates that when the Israelites in the desert asked for water, Moses became angry and called them "rebels." Instead of following Hashem's instructions to command*

the rock to produce water, Moses hit the rock. As a result, he would not be permitted to enter Eretz Yisrael (Numbers 20:2-13).

Rambam says that Moses' transgression was that he lost his temper and chastised the Israelites. However, this, too, is problematic. Moses had only one desire in life: to enter Eretz Yisrael. The Midrash says that he submitted 515 prayers to be allowed to enter Eretz Yisrael. Even if we assume that he acted improperly by becoming angry at the Israelites, did this jusify so severe a punishment?

Perhaps the answer is that Moses was not punished. Rather, during the 40 years of his leadership, Moses was constantly an advocate for the Israelites, interceding for them when they sinned. However, Moses was constantly ascending spiritually. Three times he went without food and water for 40 days. The Torah refers to Moses as "a G-dly person" (Deuteronomy 33:1), and the Midrash says that he was "half human and half angel."

It reached the point where Moses did not understand that people could have material needs, and when they demanded water, he was angry at them for even wanting water. He had no need for water, so why should they? Hashem then said that Moses had outgrown his leadership. A leader must feel the needs of his people, and if he had become so spiritual, so angelic, that he could not identify with the people, it was time to turn over the leadership to someone else.

R' Yochanan ben Zakkai told his disciples to temporarily "Go out" from their lofty spiritual status in order to identify with ordinary people. Moses was at a spiritual level from which he could not descend, even for a moment.

The Talmud says, "Do not be like servants who serve their master for reward, but be like servants who serve their master not because of the reward, and may the fear of Heaven be upon you" (*Ethics of the Fathers* 1:3). What is the relevance of "fear of Heaven" to the issue of reward?

The Maggid said that if a person is motivated by reward, he may think, "I am satisfied with the amount of reward I have already accumulated. I don't need to serve Hashem to receive more rewards." Therefore, a person should not be motivated by reward, but should serve Hashem because he fears to transgress Hashem's will. In that way, he will not be tempted to relax in his service of Hashem.

"And he [Abraham] believed in Hashem, and He [Hashem] considered this *tzeddakah* [righteousness] (*Genesis* 15:6).

The verse can be translated so that the second "he" refers to Abraham, and that Abraham considered it *tzeddakah*. The Maggid said that Abraham was grateful that Hashem had given him the intelligence to realize that there is one true G-d. Abraham was raised in a pagan environment, and his family were all idol worshipers. Abraham reasoned to the conclusion that there was only one true G-d. He believed that his ability to reject the prevailing belief and recognize the truth of Hashem was a gift from Hashem. Thus, the verse can be read, "Abraham believed in Hashem, and he considered his ability to do so to be *tzeddakah*, a kindness of Hashem to him."

וְעַתָּה אִם־שָׁמוֹעַ תִּשְׁמְעוּ בְּקֹלִי — "And now, if you will hearken to My voice" (*Exodus* 19:5). The Midrash (*Bereishis Rabbah* 21:6) states that the word וְעַתָּה — and now — refers to *teshuvah*. The Maggid said that because the Israelites had participated in the Egyptian idol worship, they did not consider themselves worthy of receiving the Torah. Hashem, therefore, told them that if they do *teshuvah*, all the sins of the past will be eradicated, and they will be worthy of receiving the Torah.

> *This is most important. A person must believe that once he has done proper teshuvah, his sins have been totally eradicated, as the prophet says, "I have erased your sins like a fog" (Isaiah 44:22). When a fog clears, no trace of it remains.*
>
> *The commentaries say that the Israelites in the desert feared going into Canaan, not because they doubted Hashem's ability to subdue the Canaanites, but rather because, remembering that they had worshiped idols in Egypt, they did not consider themselves to be worthy of Hashem doing miracles for them.*
>
> *It is a tactic of the yetzer hara to discourage a person from trying to come closer to Hashem by making him think himself unworthy of this. A person should believe that once he has done teshuvah, he has become beloved of Hashem (Rambam, Laws of Teshuvah 7:6).*

In the episode of the spies that Moses sent to scout Canaan, the Torah says that "Moses called Hoshea bin Nun Yehoshua" (*Numbers* 13:16). The *Targum Yonasan* comments, "When Moses saw Hoshea bin Nun's humility, he called him Yehoshua."

The Maggid asked, "What did Yehoshua's humility have to do with changing his name?" Furthermore, Rashi explains that the addition of the *yud* was to spell Hashem's Name, and he prayed that Hashem would spare him from the counsel of the other spies.

The Maggid cited a Midrash that says that when resurrection occurs, people will rise from the dead according to the *alef-beis*;

i.e., the first to rise will be those with the names Abraham, Aaron, Aryeh , etc., followed by those with the names Baruch, Binyamin, Ben Zion, etc. If so, why did Moses add a *yud* to Hoshea's name? Hoshea begins with *hei*, which is earlier in the *alef-beis* than *yud*, and the name change would cause a delay in his resurrection. The Maggid cited another Midrash stating that humble people will be given preference at the time of the resurrection.

Moses would not have added a *yud* if that would have delayed Yehoshua's resurrection, but, because he saw that Yehoshua was very humble, Moses realized that adding the *yud* would not affect him negatively.

If all Jews joined hands and formed one long line, it could reach up to the Throne of Glory and could bring down salvation and comfort.

Stories

A wealthy miser came to the Maggid of Kozhnitz. The Maggid said, "Tell me about the foods you eat."

The man responded, "Rebbe, I do not indulge. I get along with the bare necessities, just bread and water."

"That is very wrong," the Maggid said. "You should eat delicacies: roast meat and fine wines. If Hashem blessed you with wealth, you should indulge yourself."

The man said he would do so.

After the man left, the Maggid noticed that his chassidim were surprised by his instructions. The Maggid explained, "If a wealthy person eats delicacies, he may understand that the poor should eat bread. But if the wealthy person will eat only bread, he will think that the poor should eat rocks!"

A man in a town near Kozhnitz collected *tzeddakah*, particularly for people who had suffered financial ruin and were too embarrassed to ask for *tzeddakah*. More than once, he was treated rudely, but he accepted the insults, knowing that he was doing Hashem's will.

One day, a man came to him and poured out his bitter heart. He was destitute and could not feed his children, Moreover, his wife was sick and he could not afford the medication the doctor had prescribed. He was at his wit's end and did not know where to turn.

The *tzeddakah* collector was in a quandary. That very day he had made rounds three times to collect for the needy, and people had made it very clear to him that he was a nuisance. There was no way he could solicit them again. Yet, this poor man's plight gave him no peace. He decided he would risk people's diatribes, but he could not turn this man away.

His first stop was at a shop that sold used clothing. "You again?" the proprietor said. "How many times do you impose on people?"

Several of the proprietor's cronies were there, and they decided to have fun at this man's expense. They said, "We'll give you all the money you need, but on one condition. Here is a priest's garb. You put it on and walk through the streets for a half-hour, but don't say a word to anyone. Do that, and we'll give you the money."

The man did as they said, and as he walked through town, the townsfolk jeered at him, calling him insulting names, but he paid no mind to them. He gave the poor man the money; then collapsed and died. They buried him in the priest's garb.

Some time later, a grave was dug adjacent to the *tzeddakah* collector's grave, and they inadvertently disturbed his grave. They were shocked to find that his body was entirely intact.

The people feared that perhaps the *tzeddakah* collector had been one of the hidden *tzaddikim*, and they felt guilty that they had treated him so shabbily.

They consulted the Maggid of Kozhnitz who said, "He was not a hidden *tzaddik*, but the priest's garments, which served as the means whereby he was able to raise money for a needy family, acquired *kedushah* and served as a shield for him."

A childless couple came to the Maggid for a *berachah* that they might have a son. The Maggid said, "The Hebrew word for 'son' is בן, which has the numerical value of 52. Give me 52 gulden and I will give you a *berachah*."

"Ten gulden I can give you," the man said, "but not 52."

The Maggid said, "I'm sorry, but it must be 52."

The man went to the marketplace and returned with a bag of copper coins. "These are worth 20 gulden," he said.

The Maggid shook his head. "No, it must be 52."

The man angrily took the bag of coins and said to his wife, "Come on, let's go. Hashem will help us without the Maggid's *berachah*."

The Maggid smiled. "Hashem has already granted your wish. You thought that I have magical powers, and you did not put your trust in Hashem. Now that you have done so, you will be blessed with a child."

When the Maggid led the services on Rosh Hashanah and Yom Kippur he stood at the *amud* (pulpit) for an extended period of time, crying quietly. Then he turned toward the congregation, "Is there anyone here from Piluv?" he asked. No one from Piluv was present, but there was one person from Donwitz, a village not too far from Piluv. "Are you familiar with the town of Piluv?" the Maggid asked.

The man said, "Yes, I know the town well. I go there regularly to sell milk."

"Do you know the *poritz* (feudal lord) Kshanzi Shatrinski?"

"Yes," the man answered.

"And do you know anything about his dog?" the Maggid asked.

"Yes," the man said. "The *poritz* has a huge hound that roams around the town. It never barks at anyone."

"Do you have any idea where the *poritz* got this dog?" the Maggid asked.

"Certainly," the man said. "Everyone in Piluv knows. The *poritz* once traveled to an assembly of *poritzim*, and he paid 1800 gulden for this dog. He built it a doghouse for 200 gulden, and he feeds it 10 kilograms of meat daily."

The Maggid then turned back to the *amud* and called out, "Do you hear that, Angel Michoel?" repeating this three times, then continuing with the prayers.

After the concluding prayers on Yom Kippur, the Maggid explained. An impoverished Jew had to marry off a daughter, but he had no money for a wedding or a dowry. He went from town to town collecting *tzeddakah*, but he was very shy and never asked for much money, taking only what people gave him. Eventually he ended up in Piluv, with hardly a fraction of what he needed. He was heartbroken and sat down, weeping by the roadside.

The *poritz* and his retinue drove by, and when the *poritz* saw a man at the roadside crying, he called to him and asked him what was wrong. When the man told him about his plight, the *poritz* asked him how much he needed, and he said, "One hundred gulden." The *poritz* gave him a letter to take to his palace, instructing the palace supervisor to give the bearer 100 gulden.

The man did not take this seriously and continued his rounds among the villages. At one inn, he told the innkeeper about the *poritz* and showed him the letter.

The innkeeper said, "You fool! Take this letter to the palace, and you won't have to go begging."

He did as he was told, received 100 gulden, and returned home elated.

The Maggid said, "In heaven, this caused a furor. Satan brought serious charges against the Jews, because this man had gone around asking for help for days, and raised only a paltry sum, whereas the *poritz* promptly gave him the whole amount he needed. I could not begin the *tefillos* when there was such a sharp censure of the Jews.

"When the man told me that the *poritz* had spent 2000 gulden on his dog and the doghouse, I pointed out to the Angel Michoel that the *poritz* had not excelled in giving *tzeddakah* with his 100 gulden. Rather, he was so wealthy that money meant nothing to him, whereas the Jews from whom the man was collecting were all poor, and whatever they gave him was true *tzeddakah*. This disproved Satan's accusation, and I could continue with the prayers."

(This story is sometimes credited to Rebbe Levi Yitzchak of Berditchev.)

Rebbe Menachem Mendel of Rimanov (1745 - 1815)
Rebbe Tzvi Hirsch HaKohen (1778-1847)

Why is Rebbe Tzvi Hirsch of Rimanov included among the four masters? Because one cannot write about Rebbe Menachem Mendel without mentioning Rebbe Tzvi Hirsch. The two are inseparable. Indeed, Rebbe Menachem Mendel said that just as the Arizal said that he was sent down to this world for the sole purpose of developing his disciple Rebbe Chaim Vital, so was he, Rebbe Menachem Mendel, sent down to this world for the sole purpose of developing Rebbe Tzvi Hirsch.

Little is known about the childhood of Rebbe Menachem Mendel of Rimanov, who occupies an outstanding position in Chassidic history.

☛ There is, however, a story about his birth. His father managed an inn which belonged to a local *poritz*. One day, the *poritz* summoned him. "Moshke," he said (the father's name was Yosef, but to the *poritz*, every Jew was "Moshke"), "I know you are trustworthy and I can confide in you. I am in serious trouble, and I must leave here immediately and can never come back. I need money now, and I am ready to sell you everything I own for one-tenth of its value, but I must have the money by tomorrow. If anyone asks for me, say you know nothing. Can you get me the money?"

Reb Yosef did not have anywhere near the amount of money the *poritz* requested, but this was the opportunity of a lifetime to become fabulously wealthy. He hurried home and told his wife, and they gathered whatever gold and silver items they owned, as well as the pearls from her wedding headpiece, and sold them. Both he and his wife went to all their friends and borrowed money. Because of his reputation as a scrupulously honest person, no one denied him a loan. He raised the money the *poritz* requested, and made his way to the mansion.

On the way to the mansion, he heard loud wailing coming from a house. Curious, he went into the house to investigate. He saw a body lying on the floor, and a woman and seven children were weeping. On inquiry, the woman told him of the calamity that had befallen her. Just several hours earlier, her husband had unexpectedly died. Not only were she and the children without any source of support, but her husband owed a great deal of money, and the creditors would come and take her few possessions.

"There is nothing left for me to do but to go to the lake and drown myself and the children," she sobbed.

Reb Yosef was so moved by the woman's plight that he took the pouch of money he had intended to give the *poritz* and handed it to the woman. He then quickly left.

When Rebbe Menachem Mendel related this story, he said, "My father's act of compassion caused a great furor in heaven.

Not only could he not buy the *poritz*'s properties, not only did he dispose of every valuable thing that he owned, but he was also in deep debt to the people from whom he had borrowed. This was an unparalleled *mesiras nefesh* of *tzeddakah*, for which he should be properly rewarded.

"When Satan heard this he said, 'Not so fast! True, he did a great act of *tzeddakah*, but before he is rewarded he must be tested. I will go down to test him.'

"*Eliyahu HaNavi* then came before the Heavenly Tribunal and said, 'If he is to be tested, it cannot be by Satan, because he can put him to an impossible test. I will go down and test him.' The Heavenly Tribunal agreed to this.

"Reb Yosef, seeing that there was no pupose in continuing on to the *poritz,* and not knowing how he would tell his wife that they were now hopelessly in debt, went to the nearest village and sat in a *beis midrash. If someone sees a stranger here and invites me for a meal and gives me a place to sleep, well enough*, he thought. But he was not going to ask anyone for anything.

"After a while, an elderly man came in and gave him *Shalom*, asking what had brought him to this village. As they conversed, Reb Yosef told him everything that had transpired. The man said, 'Look, my friend, Hashem has blessed me with wealth, but if I am rich in money, I am poor in mitzvos. You desperately need money. If you sell me the reward for your mitzvah, I'll give you enough money to pay off your debts, and you will still have enough remaining for yourself.'

"Reb Yosef said, 'Since Hashem gave me the opportunity to do this mitzvah, I will not sell it for any amount of money.'

"'Very well,' the elderly man said, 'I will pay you well if you sell me half the reward for this mitzvah.'

"Again Reb Yosef refused. The man kept on bargaining, offering him the money for just a fraction of the mitzvah, but Reb Yosef would not hear of it.

"The elderly man then said, 'I am *Eliyahu HaNavi*. I was sent to test you. You not only did a mitzvah of *tzeddakah* with *mesiras nefesh*, but you also withstood the test of turning down a great deal of money for giving away only a fraction of the mitzvah. You can choose your reward from among three options: longevity for you and your wife, or extreme wealth, or to be blessed with a son who will have a very holy *neshamah*.'

"Reb Yosef said, 'We are childless. What good will long life or wealth be if I have no child?'

"*Eliyahu* then said, 'You will be blessed with a son who will illuminate the world with his Torah and *yiras Shamayim*. However, you must be ready to accept three things: you will remain poor, you will die before the child is born, and when the child is 2 years old, your wife will likewise pass away.'

"Reb Yosef said, 'For that, I must have my wife's consent.' He went home and told his wife all that had happened.

"She said, 'What good are life and wealth without a child? I agree to all three terms.'

Rebbe Menachem Mendel said, "Indeed, my mother died when I was 2, and I was raised by kind people in the community. Because my birth occurred after my father's death, they named me Menachem, in the hope that I would be consoled."

Maasei Hashem

It is a custom among some chassidim that on the *yahrzeit* (anniversary of the death) of a *tzaddik*, the *Tachanun* prayer is omitted. *Tachanun* is regularly omitted on the festivals or when there is a festive occasion in the shul, such as a *bris* or when a *chasan* during the week of his *sheva berachos* is present.

In what way is a *yahrzeit* a festive day? Apparently the practice began when chassidim would gather at the grave of a *tzaddik* on his *yahrzeit*. A meal would then be served at which the Torah teachings and events in the life of the *tzaddik* were related. It was considered a day propitious for the *zechusim* (merits) of the *tzaddik* to protect his followers, as we often say when mentioning a *tzaddik, zechuso yagen aleinu* (may his merits protect us). This evolved into a custom to omit *Tachanun* on the *yahrzeit* of a *tzaddik*.

This custom has been opposed by many authorities. It is noteworthy that the *Tzaddik* of Sanz said *Tachanun* on the *yahrzeit* of all *tzaddikim*, except for the 34th day of the *omer*, the *yahrzeit* of Rebbe Menachem Mendel of Rimanov. He said that many *neshamos* had to transmigrate a number of times until everything required of that *neshamah* was fulfilled. "The *neshamah* borne by Rebbe Menachem Mendel of Rimanov," the *Tzaddik* of Sanz said, "made its last transmigration with him, and inasmuch as it has come to its eternal rest, that day is a festive occasion."

Our first verifiable fact about Rebbe Menachem Mendel is that he studied in the yeshivah of Rebbe Shmelke of Nikolsburg. Having heard of the greatness of Rebbe Elimelech, Menachem Mendel made his way to Lizhensk, walking all the way. It was a cold winter day, and toward nightfall he stopped at an inn.

He was a handsome young man, and when he was in his room preparing to retire, the proprietress of the inn entered, intending to seduce him. Disrobed, he nevertheless ran out into the cold and raced as fast as he could. He stopped at the first hut, where he was provided with blankets and a hot drink. When he came to Lizhensk, Rebbe Elimelech greeted him, "Welcome, Yosef *HaTzaddik*," referring to the episode of Joseph who fled from the attempted seduction by the wife of Potiphar (*Genesis* 39:7-18).

☞ Rebbe Menachem Mendel wed the daughter of a man in Fristik, where he settled, devoting every minute to Torah study and *avodas Hashem*. His father-in-law was displeased and urged his daughter to request a divorce. Recognizing that her husband was a *tzaddik*, she refused, whereupon her father banished the pair from his household. The couple lived in a hut, existing on the bare minimum, often fasting when they could not afford food.

Once, the wife, knowing that her husband had not eaten a morsel for three days, asked the baker to give her a loaf of bread on credit. He refused, because she had not paid a previous debt. After she left, the baker felt regret and called her back.

"I will give you bread if you give me your share in *Olam Haba* [the Eternal World]," he said.

She thought, *I cannot allow my husband to perish of starvation,* and replied, "Give me bread and some cheese, and I will give you my share in *Olam Haba*."

She took the food to the *beis midrash* where Rebbe Menachem Mendel was learning, and broke into tears. "I gave my share in *Olam Haba* to the baker," she said.

Rebbe Menachem Mendel said, "Just before you came in, I fainted from hunger, and would have died without this food. You saved my life; that earned you your new share in *Olam Haba*."

☞ After some time, Rebbe Menachem Mendel's father-in-law felt compassion for his grandchildren and took the family into his home. Rebbe Menachem Mendel refused to eat the meat, and advised his father-in-law not to eat it because the *shochet* was a sinful person. The father-in-law paid him no heed.

One day, Rebbe Menachem Mendel told his father-in-law that he was willing to earn a living, and the two set out to the marketplace, lodging at an inn on the way.

When the other travelers at the inn saw that the proprietor was very depressed, they asked what was bothering him. He said that his daughter was having a difficult labor, and the doctors and midwives could do nothing for her.

The guests said, "That young man," pointing to Rebbe Menachem Mendel, "is a *tzaddik*. Ask him for a *berachah*."

When the proprietor approached Rebbe Menachem Mendel, the latter said, "Tell your daughter to reveal who is the father of her child."

The proprietor inquired, and told them that his daughter said her husband was the father.

Rebbe Menachem Mendel said, "Tell her that if she reveals the truth she will deliver quickly, but if she persists in denying, she may lose her life."

The woman then revealed that she had been violated by the *shochet* (ritual slaughterer). She then delivered the child, and the *shochet* was dismissed. The word that Rebbe Menachem Mendel was a great *tzaddik* spread, and soon people streamed to him for *berachos*.

Rebbe Menachem Mendel was highly esteemed by the *tzaddikim* the *Chozeh* of Lublin and the Maggid of Kozhnitz. Rebbe Mendele of Linsk, who was many years his senior, came to him for a *berachah*. Among Rebbe Menachem Mendel's disciples were Rebbe Naftali of Ropschitz; Rebbe Tzvi Elimelech of Dinov (author of *Bnei Yisasschar*); Rebbe Yechezkel Panet (author of *Mareh Yechezkel*); Rebbe Tzvi Hirsch of Zhidachov; and a number of other acknowledged *geonim*.

Rebbe Menachem Mendel was zealous in demanding adherence to the laws of *tzniyus* (modesty). He also insisted on retaining traditional Jewish garb and not emulating modern styles, especially with regard to ostentatious dress. He said that he was sure that all the *tsaros* (troubles) that Jews were experiencing were due to their emulating the dress styles of non-Jews.

> *The importance of maintaining traditional Jewish garb can be seen in the Midrash, which states that one of the merits that enabled our ancestors to be delivered from Egypt was that they maintained their traditional garb and did not dress like the Egyptians.*
>
> *Divrei Yechezkel states that Joseph wished to spread belief in Hashem in Egypt, and felt that if he dressed like the Egyptians they would be more likely to listen to him than if he appeared to be alien. When Potiphar's wife attempted to seduce him, Joseph realized that this came about because he was dressed in Egyptian clothing, indicated by the statement, "She seized him by his garment" (Genesis 39:12).*

Even today, there is a misconception that Jews should not stand out as different. Unfortunately, such ideas have resulted in the catastrophic assimilation of our times.

◈ After her marriage, the daughter of a very wealthy man dressed in very expensive clothes. The chassidim, knowing how vigorously Rebbe Menachem Mendel disapproved of this, criticized her sharply.

Her father came to Rebbe Menachem Mendel and angrily said, "What right does the Rebbe have to contradict Ezra the Scribe, who ordained that cosmetic peddlers should be free to sell their wares anywhere, so that Jewish daughters should appear attractive?"

Rebbe Menachem Mendel said, "Heaven forbid that I should contradict Ezra. However, Ezra meant that Jewish women should be attractive *to their husbands*, and not to men outside the home."

How appropriate the Rebbe's words are for our time! Many women go to work, wearing cosmetics to appear attractive, but make little effort to beautify themselves at home for their husbands!

◈ On one occasion, government officials came to Rimanov and said they were commandeering the shul to be used as a warehouse for army supplies. The community leaders came to Rebbe Menachem Mendel for suggestions how they might be able to avert this tragedy. One member of the community spoke up and said that there might be a saving grace, because the roof of the shul leaked, and if the officials became aware that the supplies may be damaged by water, they would forgo use of the shul.

Rebbe Menachem Mendel said, "What! You have allowed the shul to fall into disrepair? No wonder this has happened! Hashem has punished you for evidencing disrespect for His house. Have the roof repaired immediately and see that all necessary repairs are done, and you will see that they will withdraw their plan."

The townsfolk did as they were instructed, and when the shul was repaired, they were notified that the government no longer needed it as a warehouse.

☞ Once, when Rebbe Menachem Mendel, the Rebbe of Apta, and Rebbe Naftali of Ropschitz were together, the Rebbe of Apta said, "*Nu*, Rav of Ropschitz, how do you like the mispronunciation on Erev Yom Kippur?" Rebbe Menachem Mendel and Rebbe Naftali smiled.

Rebbe Tzvi Hirsch of Rimanov, Rebbe Menachem Mendel's aide, overheard the conversation, and he asked Rebbe Naftali what the Rebbe of Apta meant.

Rebbe Naftali told him that there had been a severe decree in heaven that many women would die of illness that year. The rabbis' efforts to abrogate the decree failed. One simple Jew, who could not read the *siddur* well, misread the *berachah* for *parnassah* (livelihood), וּבָרֵךְ שְׁנָתֵינוּ כַּשָּׁנִים הַטּוֹבוֹת לִבְרָכָה — bless our year like the best years. Instead of saying *shenaseinu* (our year), he said *neshaseinu* (our women), and he misread the conclusion of the paragraph, *mevarech hashanim* (Who blesses the years) as *mevarech hanashim* (Who blesses the women). His sincere prayer annulled the decree, and that's why the *tzaddikim* smiled.

☞ Rebbe Moshe Teitelbaum (author of *Yismach Moshe*) sent a person who was very ill to Rebbe Menachem Mendel for a *berachah*. The latter sent him back to the *Yismach Moshe,* with a message to drop his disguise and let people know that his *berachos* are effective.

"Don't send any more people to me," Rebbe Menachem Mendel wrote. "Your *berachos* are every bit as good as mine."

The man returned to the *Yismach Moshe,* received his *berachah*, and recovered.

☞ A man came to Rebbe Menachem Mendel, complaining of his *tzaros* and *kretchtzing* (sighing) loudly.

Rebbe Menachem Mendel said, "*Krechtzing* won't accomplish anything. Accept your troubles and you'll be relieved of them.

"A man carrying a heavy load was weary; he paused and was crying because of the heavy burden. Someone said to him, 'Standing there crying is not going to help. It can only make the burden heavier. Get to your destination so that you can unburden yourself.'"

☞ Rebbe Feivish of Zebarezh visited Rebbe Menachem Mendel. Before he left, he said, "Rebbe Mendel, I am already 74 and I have not done *teshuvah* yet."

Rebbe Menachem Mendel sighed. "Rebbe Feivish," he said, "I am in the same predicament."

Rebbe Feivish said, "Bless me, Rebbe Mendel, that I should merit to do *teshuvah.*"

Rebbe Menachem Mendel said, "You bless me, too, that I should merit to do *teshuvah*."

And so these two great *tzaddikim* tearfully blessed each other that they should merit to do *teshuvah*.

> *Many people are complacent, and, if they were asked whether they had done teshuvah, they might say, "For what?"*
>
> *A violin virtuoso may be upset if one note in a concerto did not come out perfectly. A beginner may play a melody totally out of tune and not be aware of it.*
>
> *If one does not feel that he must do teshuvah, it indicates how distant he is from the truth.*

☞ One Shavuos, prior to reading the Ten Commandments, Rebbe Menachem Mendel announced that anyone who had not observed the Ten Commandments should leave. Rebbe Naftali of Ropschitz promptly arose and left. When people saw that Rebbe Naftali left, they all left, and only Rebbe Menachem Mendel and Rebbe Tzvi Hirsch remained in the shul.

Rebbe Menachem Mendel sent Rebbe Tzvi Hirsch to declare that only those who had no wish to observe the Ten Commandments should have left the shul. Everyone returned.

> *We may not all be perfect, but we all may desire to be perfect.*

☞ Rebbe Menachem Mendel's son, Rebbe Nosson Yehudah, spent one Shavuos with the *Chozeh* in Lublin. On the second day of Yom Tov, the *Chozeh* asked Rebbe Nosson Yehudah, "Where is your father?" Knowing of the *Chozeh's* prophetic vision, Rebbe

Nosson Yehudah was afraid that if the *Chozeh* could not see his father, it meant that he was no longer alive.

Immediately after Yom Tov, Rebbe Nosson Yehudah left for Rimanov, and hurried home breathlessly. When he came home, he found Rebbe Menachem Mendel studying Torah. "Why are you gasping for breath?" Rebbe Menachem Mendel asked.

Rebbe Nosson Yehudah explained what had happened and why he had run home. Rebbe Menachem Mendel smiled. "The *Chozeh* was looking for me in the celestial spheres. He couldn't find me because I was in Vienna with the emperor."

Teachings

Rebbe Menachem Mendel's teachings were recorded by his disciple, Rebbe Yechezkel Panet.

For 22 years, Rebbe Menachem Mendel regularly expounded on the manna. *Tzaddikim* said that he thereby conveyed Hashem's bounty of *parnassah* to the Jews.

"Hashem said to Moses, 'Behold! I shall rain down for you food from Heaven; let the people go out and pick each day's portion on its day, so that I can test them, whether they will follow My teaching or not' "(*Exodus* 16:4).

Inasmuch as the loaves that they brought out of Egypt miraculously lasted for several weeks, why could they not have lasted until the Torah was given? Also, what is the relationship of the manna to "whether they will follow My teaching or not"?

Hashem wished to use the manna as a means to instill good *middos* within the Children of Israel in order to facilitate their observance of Torah and mitzvos. Rabbeinu Tam in *Sefer HaYashar* states that the basis of all the good *middos* are *emunah* and *bitachon* (faith and trust in Hashem), which will enable a person to fulfill the mitzvah,"Love your fellow as yourself" (*Leviticus* 19:18). The Talmud relates that when the proselyte asked Hillel to condense the Torah and teach it to him "while he is standing on one leg," Hillel told him that the essence of Torah is "Love your fellow as yourself" (*Shabbos* 31a). It is also logical that if a person loves his fellow as he loves himself, he will abstain from theft, robbery, adultery, murder, cheating, taking revenge, and other things which one's intellect dictates as being improper.

But one cannot fulfill the mitzvos related to *ahavas Yisrael* if one lacks *emunah* and *bitachon*, i.e., unless one believes wholeheartedly that Hashem conducts the world and provides every person with his needs, and that a person cannot encroach on what was destined for another person. A person who has this faith will feel secure that Hashem will provide for his needs, and consequently will not spend his days and years in the pursuit of wealth, because he believes that exerting greater effort will not bring him more than he was destined to have.

One who is accomplished in this trait will not covet what another person has nor be envious of him, because he knows that what others have was not destined for him. Even if it should appear to someone that another person is encroaching on his earnings, he will have no ill feelings toward him, because he knows that a competitor cannot take from him what was destined for him to have.

Therefore, Hashem's wisdom dictated that every person receive provisions for just that day, to teach the Children of Israel not to worry about tomorrow. Also, they were instructed not to gather more than one share of manna, one *omer* per person. As proof of this, there was a miracle that whether one gathered more than an *omer* or less than an *omer*, all found that they had just one *omer*, no more and no less. This taught them to have *emunah* and *bitachon*, which would enable them to fulfill the mitzvos of the Torah. This is the relevance of "whether they will follow My teaching or not," because the lesson of the manna is a key to observance of the Torah.

☞ A man complained to Rebbe Menachem Mendel that someone was opening a competing shop near him, and that it would detract from his *parnassah*. Rebbe Menachem Mendel said, "If you observe a horse drinking from a stream, you will note that it taps with its hoof on the ground. It does this because when it sees its reflection in the water, it thinks that there is another horse there that may drink up all the water, so it taps with its hoof to drive the other horse away.

"You should be too proud to have the mentality of a horse."

"The Children of Israel saw and said one to another, 'It is מָן הוּא כִּי לֹא יָדְעוּ־מַה הוּא (manna), for they did not know what it was" (*Exodus* 16:15). Why did the Children of Israel call it מָן ? The word מַה means "what," while the word מִי means "who." But because the manna was food from heaven, it was a spiritual food. If a person spoke to a friend one day, and met him again the next day, he would say, "Who is this?" The gathering and eating of the manna so increased their spirituality, that from day to day there was such character refinement that one did not recognize the person to whom he had spoken on the previous day. That is why they named it מָן, because it led to their asking, "Who?"

"Hashem shall bless your bread and your water, and I shall remove illness from your midst" (*Exodus* 23:25). Rebbe Menachem Mendel said that this verse also lends itself to another interpretation. "If you thank Hashem before you eat and drink, then He will remove illness from your midst."

Rabbi Menachem Mendel blessed a person, and he became exceedingly wealthy. Rebbe Naftali of Ropschitz asked, "Why did the Master give this person such great wealth?" Rebbe Menachem Mendel answered, "I blessed him with only moderate wealth, but he gave *tzeddakah* from it. The word נתן (to give) reads the same way both ways, meaning that whatever you give to *tzeddakah*, Hashem will give you even more. That is how he increased his wealth."

"You shall not hate your brother in your heart; you shall reprove your fellow" (*Leviticus* 19:17). Rebbe Menachem Mendel says that one person may have a trait that another lacks, and he may look at the other person as his inferior. Therefore, the Torah says, "Do not look down at your fellow because of what is in your heart," i.e., because he lacks a trait that you have. Rather, reprove *yourself*, for you may be lacking an admirable trait that your fellow has.

> *In the introductory prayer composed by Rebbe Elimelech of Lizhensk, it says, "Help me see only the merits of my fellows, and not their defects."*

In *davening* we say, "Hashem reigns, Hashem has reigned, Hashem shall reign for all eternity." The logical pattern is to state "past, present, future." Why, then, do we put the present before the past? Because a person must first accept the sovereignty of Hashem in the present. Only then can one think about the past and contemplate the future.

The Torah relates that the year after the Exodus, Hashem commanded the Israelites to bring the paschal offering. There were several people who were *tamei* (defiled) because they had been in contact with a dead body, and they could not bring the paschal offering. They asked Moses why they were excluded, and when Moses set their question before Hashem, Hashem dictated the law of *Pesach sheini* (second paschal offering), so that a person who was unable to bring the paschal offering on the 14th day of Nissan would be able to fulfill his obligation the following month, on the 14th day of Iyar.

The Torah says that the paschal offering should be brought *bemoadao*, in its designated time. The Talmud states that "*bemoadao*" means even in a state of *tumah* (impurity). This applies only when all of Israel is *tamei*, but if only isolated individuals are *tamei*, they cannot bring the offering "in its designated time," the 14th of Nissan, but must wait until the 14th of Iyar.

The distinction between whether all of Israel or isolated individuals are *tamei* was given by Hashem *after* these people asked why they could not bring the paschal offering. Before that, the halachah that "*bemoadao*, in its designated time" means "even in a state of *tumah*" did not make this distinction. Why, then, did these people think they were excluded from bringing the paschal offering?

Rabbi Menachem Mendel raises another question. In the *parashah* of the *Akeidah* (Binding of Isaac), the Torah says, "Abraham stretched out his hand and took the knife" (*Genesis* 22:10). It would have sufficed to say "Abraham took the knife." Why the extra words? Furthermore, the *Midrash* says that Abraham stretched out his hand "with force." Why was force necessary?

The Talmud says that Abraham fulfilled all the mitzvos of the Torah (*Yoma* 28b). How could he have observed the mitzvos before they were given?

Rabbi Menachem Mendel pointed out that the *sefarim* say that 248 anatomical parts of the human body correspond to the 248 positive mitzvos, and 365 anatomical parts of the human body correspond to the 365 halachic prohibitions. Thus, every part of the body relates either to a mitzvah or to a prohibition.

Abraham had developed so high a spiritual level and such total devotion to Hashem that every part of his body wished to serve Hashem. The parts of the body that corresponded to the 248 mitzvos and 365 prohibitions were automatically attracted to doing that particular mitzvah and avoiding that particular prohibition.

The *Midrash* says that it was never Hashem's will that Isaac should be brought as an offering. Rather, it was a test of Abraham's devotion, as the Torah says, "Hashem tested Abraham" (*Genesis* 22:1). Abraham, however, thought that this was what Hashem wanted. When he began to take the knife, his hand resisted, because the hand would do only what Hashem wanted. Therefore, Abraham had to forcibly stretch out his hand, to overcome its resistance.

The people who consulted Moses about the paschal offering were great *tzaddikim*. They assumed that "*bemoadao*, in its designated time, even when *tamei*" applied to them as well. When they tried to bring the paschal offering, they found that "they were *unable*" to do so (*Numbers* 9:6), i.e., they felt a strong resistance, much like Abraham did, and they realized that something was wrong. Moses then revealed to them that it was Hashem's will that individuals who are *tamei* should not bring the paschal offering on the 14th day of Nissan, which explains why they felt "unable" to do so.

Rebbe Menachem Mendel instructed his followers that when they return from a trip, they should stop to eat before going home, because if they enter the house when they are hungry, they are likely to be irritable and may speak crossly to members of the family.

Rebbe Menachem Mendel instructed his followers that when they have a guest at the table, they should take a bite of food or drink before serving the guest. He cited the Talmud that resolves an apparent contradiction between two verses. One verse says, "The earth and its fullness belongs to Hashem" (*Psalms* 24:1), while another verse says, "the earth He has given to mankind" (ibid. 115:16). The Talmud says that before one recites a *berachah*, everything belongs to Hashem, but after one has recited a *berachah*, one acquires rights to the item.

Therefore, Rebbe Menachem Mendel said, if one serves the guest before reciting a *berachah*, he is giving the guest something that does not belong to the host. Once one has recited a *berachah*, it becomes his property and he may give it to others.

A person should be particularly cautious, when doing a mitzvah or a good deed, to carry it out to its completion. People often discover all manner of obstacles that deter them from completing the mitzvah. This is because the *yetzer hara* makes a special effort to undermine completing the mitzvah. If one persists with the desire to complete it, Hashem will help him do so.

> *In Mesilas Yesharim's chapter on Zerizus (diligence), Ramchal points out that one must have zerizus both when beginning a mitzvah and along the way. It is not uncommon for a person to begin something with much enthusiasm, but gradually lose interest as one progresses. Ramchal especially warns about procrastination, using the strong language that "there is no other danger as great as procrastination." If a person decides not to do something, one does not deceive himself. A procrastinator deceives himself, thinking, "I will do it, but not just now," and believes this to be true, whereas it is nothing other than an avoidance of something one does not want to do but does not want to admit it.*

Rebbe Menachem Mendel said that he saw in an ancient *sefer* that the reason the Chazal did not prescribe a *berachah* for the mitzvah of *tzeddakah* is because a *berachach* must be said with *simchah*, and most people are not happy when they have to give away their money.

In referring to *tzeddakah*, Rebbe Menachem Mendel cited the Talmud that says that when a person gives *tzeddakah* to a poor person when he is in need, Hashem will answer his prayers (*Yevamos* 63a). The Rebbe asked, "What is meant by 'a poor person when he is in need'? A poor person is *always* in need!

"The Talmud means that when a person gives *tzeddakah* to a poor person when he, *the donor*, is himself in need, yet he gives away from his meager possessions to help another poor person, that is indeed a great mitzvah."

At Minchah on Shabbos, we recite the verse, "As for me, let my prayer to You, Hashem, be at an opportune time. O G-d, in Your abundant kindness, answer me with the truth of Your salvation" (*Psalms* 69:14). The implication is that Shabbos Minchah is a propitious time for prayer. What is so special about this time?

Rebbe Menachem Mendel said that the Torah says about Creation, "And there was evening and there was morning, one day" (*Genesis* 1:5). The first day of Creation, therefore, was Sunday, and Creation began on the eve of Sunday ('And there was evening,' ibid.). Hashem's will to create the world, therefore, preceded Sunday eve, which would correspond to our late Shabbos afternoon, which is the time of Minchah. Shabbos Minchah is an opportune time, because that is when Hashem willed to create the world."

Rebbe Menachem Mendel said that idle talk before Shacharis (morning service) weakens one's *yiras Shamayim*.

⇜ *Rebbe Tzvi Hirsch HaKohen of Rimanov*

As noted earlier, one cannot write about Rebbe Menachem Mendel without mentioning Rebbe Tzvi Hirsch. The two are inseparable.

Rebbe Tzvi Hirsch is one of most fascinating personalities in Chassidic lore. He is generally referred to as Reb Hirsch *Meshores* (attendant). The reason for this will soon become evident.

Rebbe Tzvi Hirsch was one of the most highly respected *tzaddikim*. The great gaon, the *Tzaddik* of Sanz, considered himself a student of Rebbe Tzvi Hirsch. Ironically, Rebbe Tzvi Hirsch was often thought of as being unlearned, and his enormous erudition was well concealed.

Rebbe Tzvi Hirsch was born in Dombrow, to parents who were devout but simple people. When Rebbe Tzvi Hirsch was 10, a virulent epidemic swept through the community, and he was orphaned of both parents in one day. A distant cousin adopted the child, but in a matter of several months the cousin became impoverished and could not afford to feed an extra mouth. Young Tzvi Hirsch was then apprenticed to a tailor who was to teach him the trade of needle and thread. Tzvi Hirsch was to earn his room and board by running errands, bringing in firewood, and doing other chores.

The tailor was a gentle and devout person, who tried to instill in Tzvi Hirsch the character traits appropriate for a Jew. Tzvi Hirsch was obedient. He *davened* with great fervor, even though he did not know the exact meaning of all the Hebrew words. He was forever inspired by his father's last words, "Never forget that you are a *Kohen*, and that 'the lips of a *Kohen* should safeguard knowledge'" (*Malachi* 52:7). Whenever Tzvi Hirsch was free from doing chores, he did not join the other children in play, but would recite *Tehillim*. However, he did not have the opportunity to further his knowledge of Scripture and Talmud.

Tzvi Hirsch was envious of the children who were privileged to learn Torah and would fantasize that if only he had the opportunity to learn Torah, he might even become a *tzaddik*! But then he castigated himself. What right did he have to indulge in such grandiose delusions? He was nothing but a tailor's apprentice, and even this position was granted him only because people felt compassion for an orphan. But who was he really? A nothing, and a rather homely nothing at that. More than once he was the butt of the taunts of other children who mocked this strange child.

One day, the news spread through town that the renowned *tzaddik*, Rebbe Moshe of Pshevorsk, was planning to travel through the village, and Tzvi Hirsch was gripped by a desire to feast his eyes on the *tzaddik*. But Rebbe Moshe was a very private person, carefully guarded by his *gabbaim* from contact with people. There was just no way that Tzvi Hirsch, a lowly tailor's apprentice, could get to see the *tzaddik*.

But the desire to see the *tzaddik* gave Tzvi Hirsch no peace, and he came upon a bright idea. Before dawn, he entered the deserted *mikveh* (bathhouse) through an open window, and concealed himself under one of the benches. He lay there, silent as a statue, and watched how the *tzaddik's gabbai* helped him. The aide then left the room. Tzvi Hirsh emerged from his hiding place and watched the *tzaddik* immerse in the water. The boy then quickly returned to his hiding place, and, after the *tzaddik* had left the room, Tzvi Hirsch hurriedly undressed and jumped into the water, hoping to have at least indirect contact with the *tzaddik* by bathing in the water in which the *tzaddik* had purified himself.

Tzvi Hirsch felt that a transformation was taking place, as if the holiness of the *tzaddik* was entering his pores. His *davening* that day was markedly different, because whereas he had previously *davened* with silent tears, he could now not contain his voice and he cried aloud, often gesticulating wildly. The people in shul looked upon him as deranged. *Who does this young boy think he is, acting as if he was being carried away by the fervor of his prayers?* Tzvi Hirsch tried to subdue his voice and his waving hands, but to no avail. And what was the substance of his prayer? *"Ribono shel Olam!* Open my mind and teach me Your Torah!" And then he would cry, feeling that his prayers were futile. One does not acquire knowledge of Torah by prayer, but by diligent study. However, he was busy all day as the tailor's apprentice and there was scant time to study Torah.

Perhaps because he could no longer abide the gibes of the townsfolk or perhaps because he hoped he would find a better opportunity to study Torah elsewhere, Tzvi Hirsch told the tailor that he was leaving.

"Where will you go?" the tailor asked.

"Perhaps to Fristik, the home of the great *tzaddik* Rebbe Menachem Mendel. Perhaps there I will find a way to learn Torah."

"*Oy, oy,* Tzvi Hirsch," the tailor said. "I'm afraid you are more motivated by laziness than by a desire to learn. I am trying to make a tailor out of you, so that you'll be able to support yourself."

But there was no stopping Tzvi Hirsch. The tailor gave him a few coins, and with just some bread and the clothes on his back, Tzvi Hirsch began the long trek to Fristik.

Every now and then, when a passing wagon offered him a lift, Tzvi Hirsch was able to rest his legs. Sometimes the travelers shared their food with him. True, he had no father, but the Father of all orphans was looking after him, providing him with compassionate people who offered him transport and food.

After several days, he arrived in Fristik, and soon found his way to the *beis midrash* of the *tzaddik*, Rebbe Menachem Mendel. He told the people who greeted him that he was an orphan, ignorant of Torah but anxious to learn, and that he was hopeful he could find some way to support himself and learn Torah, and perhaps do some chores for the *tzaddik*.

The people felt pity for the young boy, who obviously was not aware that few people had access to the *tzaddik*, who was a very frail person, tormented by much pain. The child appeared sincere, and they made it their business to give him food and to allow him to sleep on a bench in the *beis midrash*. Tzvi Hirsch tried to study, and was overjoyed when someone would take a few minutes to teach him something of the *Chumash* and *Mishnah*. At other times, he would try to learn on his own, and would frequently question the others who were learning there, asking them to explain the meaning of a word or phrase.

Tzvi Hirsch frequented the *tzaddik's* environs, and he noticed the *shamash* (sexton), an elderly man, chopping wood for the fire. Tzvi Hirsch approached the *shamash* and offered to chop the wood for him. The *shamash* gladly accepted, but Tzvi Hirsch was allowed to carry the wood only to the door. Gradually, Tzvi Hirsch won the confidence and even the affection of the *shamash,* who thereafter allowed him to carry the wood into the house.

Tzvi Hirsch also offered to kindle the fire, but the *shamash* explained that this was impossible. "The *tzaddik* is very sickly and sensitive," he explained. "The fire must be made just so, because both inadequate heat and excessive heat are very irritating to the *tzaddik*. And moist wood must be avoided, because any smoke can trigger a life-threatening cough."

Tzvi Hirsch understood, and carefully observed how the *shamash* arranged the wood and kindled the fire. Again, his persistence paid off, and after several months the *shamash* yielded to the boy's entreaties and allowed him to light the stove.

Tzvi Hirsch was overjoyed by this opportunity, and carefully selected the wood, arranging it perfectly for a steady flame, setting each piece of wood in place accompanied by a verse from *Tehillim* that he had memorized, and thanking Hashem for the privilege to be of service to the *tzaddik*. Soon Tzvi Hirsch was tending the stove regularly, and this gave him the coveted opportunity to occasionally get a glimpse of the *tzaddik* when the door to the study was ajar.

Every day, the *shamash* prepared the *tzaddik's* bed. The *tzaddik* refused to sleep on a regular bed, having vowed to deprive himself of this comfort as long as Hashem's people were in exile and the Divine Presence was absent from Jerusalem. The *tzaddik* slept on a mat of straw, supported by ropes stretched across a wooden frame. Tzvi Hirsch watched how the *shamash* would carefully arrange the straw, and when asked to be allowed the privilege of preparing the *tzaddik's* bed, Tzvi Hirsch was again told this was impossible. The straw had to be meticulously arranged so that the frail body of the *tzaddik* would rest comfortably for the brief period that the *tzaddik* allowed himself to sleep.

But one day, the *shamash* took ill, and had no option but to ask Tzvi Hirsch to make the *tzaddik's* bed, cautioning him to do it exactly as he had seen him do it. Tzvi Hirsch thanked Hashem for this privilege, and as he carefully arranged the straw, he recited *Tehillim* with great devotion, praying to Hashem that his efforts succeed in giving the *tzaddik* his much-needed rest.

The following day, Rebbe Menachem Mendel asked the *shamash* who had prepared the bed the day before. The *shamash* began excusing himself, explaining that he had taken sick.

"I never slept so peacefully before," Rebbe Menachem Mendel said. "My dreams were heavenly, and when I awoke to the midnight prayers, I felt the holiness of *Tehillim* inspiring me."

It is well known that *tzaddikim* were able to sense spirituality in inanimate objects. Rebbe Menachem Mendel had thus sensed the love and devotion to Hashem that Tzvi Hirsch had infused into the bed, and told the *shamash* that henceforth Tzvi Hirsch was to make his bed every day. Gradually, Tzvi Hirsch took on additional duties, even helping the *tzaddik* don his clothes.

Years later, Rebbe Tzvi Hirsch married, and he was in the *beis midrash* at the usual early hour on the morning after the wedding, sweeping the floor. Rebbe Nosson Yehudah, the *tzaddik's* son, mentioned to his father that it was very inappropriate for a *chasan* to be doing this during his week of *sheva berachos*.

Rebbe Menachem Mendel said, "So? I'm glad you told me. I was worried how I would be able to *daven* if Tzvi Hirsch was not here to sweep the floor. You see, when Tzvi Hirsch sweeps the floor, he sweeps away all the *chitzonim* [non-*kedushah* elements] that find their way everywhere."

Tzvi Hirsch eventually assumed all the responsibilities of the *shamash*, who was approaching the age of retirement. The zenith of joy came when Tzvi Hirsch was allowed to assist the *tzaddik* don his second pair of *tefillin* after Shacharis. The *tzaddik's* intense prayers left him so exhausted that he did not have enough energy to put on the second pair of *tefillin* on his own. Tzvi Hirsch now became the *tzaddik's* constant attendant and never left his side, earning the appellation, "*Hirsch Meshores*" (Hirsch the attendant), by which he is known to this very day.

When Rebbe Menachem Mendel moved from Fristik to Rimanov, his faithful attendant accompanied him.

The joy of serving the great *tzaddik* was so great that it obscured all the gibes directed at Tzvi Hirsch. He was still ridiculed for his loud and frenzied manner of praying, and as his every move began to resemble those of Rebbe Menachem Mendel, he was denounced for the audacity of someone who was a boor daring to mimic the great *tzaddik,* as though he, too, were a *tzaddik*. Even Rebbe Menachem Mendel's favorite disciple, Rebbe Naftali of Ropschitz, did not lose the opportunity to denounce the upstart. But Tzvi Hirsch bore all the insults in silence. He had attained the aspiration of his lifetime, and nothing else mattered. Tzvi Hirsch was secretly becoming a scholar, but he continued to conceal this by frequently asking people to translate rather simple phrases for him.

Rebbe Menachem Mendel saw to it that Tzvi Hirsch took a wife, but alas, misfortune haunted the young couple: their children all died in early infancy. Yet, Tzvi Hirsch was not dejected. Even these grave personal losses did not detract from the joy of being the *tzad-*

dik's personal attendant. Tzvi Hirsch's wife, however, could not share in his ecstasy, and wept before the *tzaddik*. Why was she being punished so, to lose all her children?

Rebbe Menachem Mendel called in his attendant. "Hirsch," the *tzaddik* said, "what is the point of your bringing down *neshamos* that are so holy and spiritual that they cannot adjust to the grossness of this physical world?"

☞ The story of Tzvi Hirsch's marriage is an epic all its own. Because he was believed to be totally ignorant of Torah and had no family, no *shidduch* could be found for him. Rebbe Menachem Mendel asked that it be revealed to him who Tzvi Hirsch's destined *zivug* (mate) was, and when he learned who it was and where she lived, Rebbe Menachem Mendel maneuvered matters to arrange this marriage.

In the presence of all assembled, Rebbe Menachem Mendel shouted at Tzvi Hirsch, "Get out of my house, you *ganiff* [thief]! From the day you entered my house you have been stealing from me. Now get out!"

Word quickly spread that Rebbe Menachem Mendel had banished his trusted attendant because he was a thief, and all doors were closed to him. When he tried to enter a *beis midrash*, he was thrown out. He had no choice but to leave town, although he had no idea where to go. He trekked along the road until a passing wagoneer gave him a ride and dropped him off at the first inn.

The proprietor had gone to the city, and his wife and daughter were left in charge of the inn. Tzvi Hirsch sat near the stove to warm up from the frigid weather, made worse by a raging blizzard. The propeietress asked him if he wanted something to eat. Tzvi Hirsch told her that he had not eaten all day, but had no money. The proprietress took pity on him and served him a light repast. He asked whether he could sleep on a bench in the inn and he would leave at daybreak, and she agreed to this.

The proprietress told him that she and her daughter were going to their residence. She told Tzvi Hirsch that if anyone knocked at the inn's front door, he was to summon her. She would then go out and see who it was, because at times undesirable people arrived. If she saw that they were decent people, she would open the inn for them.

Several hours later, there was a loud knocking at the door. Tzvi Hirsch asked who was there, and was told that they were a group of merchants en route from the market. The coachman had lost his bearings because of the blizzard, and they needed a place to stay overnight. Tzvi Hirsch summoned the proprietress, and she went out to see them.

She was convinced that they were decent people and opened the inn for them. They said that they were wealthy merchants and could pay well for food and drink. The horses were stabled and fed. The proprietress and her daughter served the merchants, and they drank to intoxication. Tzvi Hirsch, meanwhile, went to sleep on the bench while the company made merry, singing and dancing. Their spirits were high and the drink only escalated their gaiety.

They asked who the young man was, and the proprietress told them that he was a poor young man to whom she had given food and shelter. One of the merchants, well under the influence of alcohol, said, "We are having such a great time here. It would be even better if we had something to celebrate, like a wedding. Let's put on a play. This young *shlepper* can be the *chasan,* and this young woman can be the *kallah.*"

Everyone thought this was a brilliant idea. They fashioned a *chuppah* (wedding canopy) out of several tablecloths and went through a mock wedding ceremony.

"Now that we've had a wedding," they said, "we must have a wedding feast." The proprietress brought them more food and drink. At dawn, they paid the proprietress for their fare and left.

Tzvi Hirsch believed that all this was something that the *tzaddik* had contrived, and that in the morning he could return to Rimanov. In the morning the innkeeper returned, and when he saw all the dishes and bottles on the table, he inquired what had occurred. His wife told him about the group of wealthy merchants that had been there all night.

Tzvi Hirsch finished *davening* in the morning, and went over to the proprietor, saying, "Mazal tov!"

"Mazal tov for what?" the proprietor asked.

"We had a wedding here last night, and I married your daughter."

The wife then told her husband about the mock ceremony they had performed.

Tzvi Hirsch said, "To me it was not a mock ceremony. I was serious when I married your daughter."

The daughter said, "See, here is the ring he gave me."

The proprietor was taken aback. He knew that the young man said that he was serious and that to him it was not a mock wedding. The more the innkeeper heard about what had happened, the more he realized that he was in trouble. His daughter would have to be released from this marriage by a *get* (halachic divorce). At first he took a conciliatory approach, telling Tzvi Hirsch that he could not allow his daughter to be married to a mediocre indigent, and seeing that he was poor, he would give him a handsome gift to accompany him to the Rav for a *get*.

When Tzvi Hirsch said that he would not give a *get*, the proprietor's attitude changed. He called in some of his servants and threatened to beat Tzvi Hirsch if he did not give her a *get*. When Tzvi Hirsch refused, the innkeeper made good on his threat and they beat him severely. But Tzvi Hirsch did not yield. He believed that this was his true *zivug*, and that the *tzaddik* had somehow orchestrated the events.

Tzvi Hirsch tried to avoid a beating by heading toward the door, but the servants blocked his exit. "You are not going to run away and leave my daughter an *agunah* [a married woman who has not been released by a *get*]!" the father shouted. Tzvi Hirsch was thrown into a locked room in the cellar. Every day he was given a bare ration of food, and beaten anew, but Tzvi Hirsch was adamant: No *get*!

After several days, the proprietor said, "If we go to the *tzaddik* in Rimanov and he orders you to give a *get*, will you do so?"

Tzvi Hirsch readily agreed to this. The father-in-law had Tzvi Hirsch bound with ropes to make sure that he could not escape, and they put him on a wagon and headed for Rimanov.

Rebbe Menachem Mendel knew via his *ruach hakodesh* (Divine intuition) what had happened. He ordered all the residents of Rimanov to close their shops and put on their fine Shabbos clothes, and follow him to the outskirts of Rimanov. The wagon with the proprietor, his wife, and daughter approached, followed by a wagon in which Tzvi Hirsh lay bound under the eyes of two guards. As the wagons entered Rimanov, Rebbe Menachem Mendel ordered everyone to exclaim, "Mazal tov!" and instructed them to accompany the wagons with song all the way to his residence.

When they reached the *tzaddik's* home, he dispersed the crowd, telling them to return in the evening for *simchas chasan v'kallah* (celebrating with the newlywed couple).

The proprietor could not understand what was happening, and when they entered the *tzaddik's* home, he began pleading with the *tzaddik* to have mercy and order the young man to give a *get*. If the Rebbe would not do so, they would take the matter before the civil authorities.

Rebbe Menachem Mendel then told them, "This young man is not a simple *bachur* [lad]. He is my faithful attendant. He has a *neshamah* of the highest magnitude. When his time comes to be revealed, he will shine bright as the midday sun and will be a leader in Israel. He will have disciples who, too, will shed their light on the world. You should know that just as the Arizal was sent down to this world to develop his disciple, Rebbe Chaim Vital, so, too, was I sent down to develop this young man.

"I prayed to be shown who his true *zivug* is, and I was told that it was your daughter. I chased him from my home so that he should find his way to your inn. The travelers that night were heavenly angels in human form. Your daughter is fortunate to have so great a *tzaddik* as her husband. Now you must ask his forgiveness for having dealt with him so cruelly."

At night, when the townsfolk gathered to celebrate *simchas chasan v'kallah*, Rebbe Menachem Mendel said, "When I said that Tzvi Hirsch is a *ganiff*, I was not lying. All the high spiritual levels that I worked so hard to achieve, he 'stole' from me. There is nothing I could hide from him. None of my disciples have taken from me what Tzvi Hirsch has."

Inasmuch as the "merchants" at the inn were angels in human form, they could not be valid *eidim* (witnesses). The wedding ceremony was repeated with great joy.

Emes V'yatziv, citing *Otzar Hasipurim*

The animosity of Rebbe Menachem Mendel's followers toward Tzvi Hirsch continued to grow, and one time, Rebbe Naftali of Ropschitz asked the *tzaddik* to dismiss Tzvi Hirsch. Rebbe Menachem Mendel shook his head. "It says in *Tehillim,* 'He who walks the way of perfect innocence, he shall serve me' [*Psalms* 101:6], and that is Tzvi Hirsch." Eventually, they prevailed upon the *tzaddik's* son, Rebbe Nosson Yehudah, to ask for Tzvi Hirsch's dismissal, and after 25 years of loyal service, Tzvi Hirsch was let go.

It is related that Rebbe Menachem Mendel had a dream in which he saw the crown being removed from his head and placed on the head of Tzvi Hirsch. He told the dream to Rebbe Naftali, who felt that this indicated that the time had come for Rebbe Menachem Mendel to leave this world and for Tzvi Hirsch to succeed him.

This was the reason for his insisting on Tzvi Hirsch's dismissal — to prolong Rebbe Menachem Mendel's life.

It was not too long after this that the *tzaddik*, Rebbe Menachem Mendel, left this world. (Rebbe Tzvi Hirsch said that had he remained, the *tzaddik* would have lived longer as a result of Tzvi Hirsch's entreaties.) It is related that shortly before his death, Rebbe Naftali asked for the *tzaddik's* blessing, which the *tzaddik* gave by placing his left hand on Rebbe Naftali's head.

"And the right hand is for whom?" Rebbe Naftali asked.

"For Tzvi Hirsch," the *tzaddik* replied.

After Rebbe Menachem Mendel's death, his son, Rebbe Nosson Yehudah, fearing that he would be pressured to assume his father's mantle of leadership, fled Rimanov to parts unknown. Tzvi Hirsch wished to avoid any suspicion that he had aspirations of inheriting the leadership; he left to join the court of Rebbe Naftali of Ropschitz, in spite of his awareness that the latter had been his adversary. Rebbe Naftali's court was graced by disciples who were Torah scholars of the highest rank, such as Rebbe Chaim, the *Tzaddik* of Sanz.

In this company, Tzvi Hirsch retained his identity as one who barely had the elementary knowledge of an advanced *cheder* student. Rebbe Naftali was cordial to Tzvi Hirsch, but that was about all. However, when Rebbe Naftali's daughter fell ill, she asked his disciples to pray for her. Rebbe Tzvi Hirsch said that if she would give him a large sum of money to distribute as *tzeddakah*, she would recover. The other disciples told this to Rebbe Naftali, who said, "If Reb Tzvi Hirsch asks for that, give it to him." She gave him the sum and she recovered.

It is related that when Rebbe Naftali's son asked his father why he did not show greater recognition to Rebbe Tzvi Hirsch (as we will henceforth refer to him), Rebbe Naftali replied, "Rebbe Tzvi Hirsch reaches the highest levels in Heaven because of his profound humility. I do not dare jeopardize that."

Rebbe Tzvi Hirsch remarried after his wife's death, and his second wife bore him a daughter. It is not known how he supported his family during the 12 years he spent in Ropschitz, but this much is certain: They subsisted far below the poverty level. Yet, Rebbe Tzvi Hirsch was happy with his lot, even when his daughter became eligible for a *shidduch,* and, without a dowry, prospects for marriage were dim.

But Rebbe Tzvi Hirsch felt that this was Hashem's worry rather than his. A person's responsibility is to advance himself spiritually, because that is the one area that Hashem has left to man's free choice. How much money a person will earn is ordained by Hashem. Why waste time on what Hashem will take care of, when one has so much yet to learn in Torah?

☞ One day, a chassid of Rebbe Naftali came to the Rebbe in a state of panic. He was a wealthy merchant whose business had previously prospered, but in recent months things had taken a sharp turn downward. Although he still had some money, he was fearful that, unless the trend reversed, he would be totally bankrupt before long. He had a large family and many obligations, and he was devastated by the prospect of becoming impecunious. He pleaded for a *berachah* — nay, a promise — that his fortunes would improve.

Rebbe Naftali told him that a *berachah* was certainly in order, but that no one could make a promise. He reminded the merchant that a rebbe is not G-d and cannot control the world. The merchant begged and wept and would not be consoled with just a *berachah*. He insisted on an assurance.

"Hear me," Rebbe Naftali said. "Reb Tzvi Hirsch says that sincere prayer and abundant *tzeddakah* can reverse the harshest of Divine decrees. Perhaps that is what you should do."

"Hirsch?" the chassid asked. "You mean Hirsch *Meshores* out there?" He promptly rushed out to the *beis midrash*, threw himself at Rebbe Tzvi Hirsch's feet, and pleaded for help.

Rebbe Tzvi Hirsch believed that Hashem would somehow provide for his daughter's dowry, and he believed that this man was the vehicle that Hashem had chosen.

"My daughter is in need of a dowry," he said. "I need 50 silver pieces. By virtue of this mitzvah, Hashem will bless you."

The merchant was stunned. "Fifty silver pieces? You jest, Reb Hirsch. That is a huge amount. Five pieces, even 10 pieces is possible, but 50 is far too great a sum." But Rebbe Tzvi Hirsch stood his ground, and finally the man brought him 50 silver pieces. No sooner had he given Rebbe Tzvi Hirsch the money than he felt a heavy burden had been lifted from his heart, and he left the *beis midrash* in a spirit of elation.

Needless to say, from that day on the merchant's business prospered, and the word soon spread that Rebbe Tzvi Hirsch's *berachah* had borne fruit. People began relating to him with much greater reverence. Soon afterward, Rebbe Naftali passed away, and Rebbe Tzvi Hirsch returned to Rimanov.

Once when Rebbe Tzvi Hirsch traveled though the town of Sanik, a family came to him, sobbing that the husband and father was in a coma due to a heart-and-lung condition and the doctors had given up hope. They asked Rebbe Tzvi Hirsch to visit the patient.

When Rebbe Tzvi Hirsch saw the patient, he asked, "Do you recognize me?" but the patient did not respond. Rebbe Tzvi Hirsch then asked everyone to leave the room except for his *shamash*, lit his pipe, and sat at the patient's bedside, meditating. Just then the doctor walked in.

Detecting smoke in the patient's room, he shouted, "Who is smoking in here? That is killing the patient!" and left angrily.

Shortly afterward, Rebbe Tzvi Hirsch again asked the patient, "Do you recognize me?"

The patient whispered, "You are the Rebbe's *meshores.*"

Rebbe Tzvi Hirsch then left to Linsk, and on his return home he again stopped in Sanik. At this time the patient was up and about, and he welcomed Rebbe Tzvi Hirsch as "my Rebbe." The story of this man's cure soon spread.

Nothing excites people like a report that there is a *tzaddik* whose *berachos* are fulfilled, and news of the incidents of the merchant who had prospered after Rebbe Tzvi Hirsch's *berachah* and of the terminally ill patient who had recovered spread rapidly. People who had suspected that Rebbe Tzvi Hirsch's fervent prayers were but an act now concluded that they had made a grave mistake, and that for years they had not appreciated that a *tzaddik* was in their midst.

They began flocking to Rebbe Tzvi Hirsch for *berachos* for cures for the sick, for children for the childless, and lo! Rebbe Tzvi Hirsch's *berachos* merited results. And wonder upon wonder! Rebbe Tzvi Hirsch began expounding on the Torah and pearls of wisdom poured from his lips. It was not the fervent prayer that had been an act! Rebbe Tzvi Hirsch had secretly become a scholar, but had led people to believe that he was ignorant.

☞ Every *Erev Rosh Chodesh*, Rebbe Menachem Mendel would send messengers to all the shops to check their weights, ensuring that their measurements were accurate. He sent Rebbe Tzvi Hirsch (who was then known only as the *tzaddik's meshores*), together with another person, to check the weights and measures. When they came into a shop with a proprietor who was something of a scholar, they found one measure that was inaccurate. Rebbe Tzvi Hirsch brought this to the attention of the proprietor, who said, "I never use that one."

Rebbe Tzvi Hirsch said, "The halachah is that you may not have an inaccurate measure in your possession, even if it is only used for garbage."

The proprietor said, "So! The *meshores* is dictating halachah!"

Rebbe Tzvi Hirsch took the measure and crushed it.

When they returned, Rebbe Menachem Mendel asked if everything was in order. Rebbe Tzvi Hirsch did not mention the episode, fearing that the *tzaddik* might punish the proprietor, but the man accompanying him reported the incident.

Rebbe Menachem Mendel sent his *shamash* to call everyone but that shopkeeper to an emergency session in the shul.

In the shul, Rebbe Menachem Mendel delivered a lecture on the subject of honest weights and measures. The proprietor, hearing about this, realized that this speech was the result of his misdemeanor. He came to Rebbe Menachem Mendel to ask for forgiveness and accept chastisement. Rebbe Menachem Mendel said, "You question Reb Tzvi Hirsch's ability to quote halachah? I doubt if the head of your yeshivah in Heaven is as knowledgeable in Torah as is Reb Tzvi Hirsch."

The entire time, Rebbe Tzvi Hirsch was noted to be mumbling to himself. When asked what he was doing, he said that he was praying that the proprietor not be punished for provoking Rebbe Menachem Mendel.

At the *yahrzeit* of Rebbe Naftali, when his disciples gathered, Rebbe Nosson Yehudah, son of the saintly Rebbe Menachem Mendel, told the group that his father had said that Rebbe Tzvi Hirsch was a true *tzaddik*. Soon the disciples of Rebbe Naftali, among them noted Chassidic masters and accomplished Talmudic scholars, began making pilgrimages to the new rebbe of Rimanov, Reb Hirsch *Meshores*.

☞ The *tzaddik* Rebbe Shimon of Yaroslav visited Rebbe Tzvi Hirsch, and Friday evening Rebbe Tzvi Hirsch asked Rebbe Shimon to lead the *kabbalas Shabbos* services. At the end of *Lechah Dodi*, before the verse *Bo'i B'shalom*, Rebbe Shimon backed away from the pulpit and asked Rebbe Tzvi Hirsch to recite the last verse. Rebbe Tzvi Hirsch began singing and dancing, and the entire congregation joined in. Someone asked Rebbe Shimon why he had not concluded *Lechah Dodi* himself.

Rebbe Shimon said, "I knew that the Heavenly angels were desirous of hearing Rebbe Tzvi Hirsch sing *Bo'i B'shalom*, so I wanted to fulfill their wish."

☞ It was Rebbe Tzvi Hirsch's practice that when he gave someone a *berachah* for a son, he asked to be invited to the *pidyon haben* (redemption of the first-born son). He was invited to the town of Kartushin on one such occasion, and everyone gathered for a gala *seudah* (meal). When Rebbe Tzvi Hirsch was leaving, the people escorted him to his coach, and one person mentioned that the town was experiencing a water shortage.

Rebbe Tzvi Hirsch took his cane, drew a circle on the ground with the tip, and said, "Let them dig here." When they dug at that spot, they found a spring that produced abundant water.

Some distance away, the star of Rebbe Israel of Rizhin had risen, and the Chassidic world was ablaze with admiration for this *tzaddik*. Rebbe Tzvi Hirsch longed to meet the Rebbe of Rizhin. It is related that Rebbe Tzvi Hirsch's *shamash* traveled to the Rizhiner to ask him to pray for Rebbe Tzvi Hirsch's remaining child, that he not lose her, Heaven forbid, as he lost his first 14 children.

When the *shamash* told the Rizhiner who he was, the Rizhiner arose and said, "The *tzaddik* Rebbe Tzvi Hirsch of Rimanov! Why, he is a pillar of holy fire!" He then asked, "Does your Rebbe travel a great deal?" The *shamash* said that the Rebbe rarely traveled. The Rizhiner said, "Not so! He constantly travels, even on Shabbos and Yom Tov, to places in Heaven so high that angels cannot reach them. How I would love to see him."

When the *shamash* told Rebbe Tzvi Hirsch that the Rizhiner was longing to see him, he traveled to Sadigura, where the Rizhiner then resided. Groups of chassidim joined him on the way, and he arrived at the head of a throng. The Rizhiner accorded Rebbe Tzvi Hirsch the greatest honors, and told his chassidim that Rebbe Tzvi Hirsch can reach those heights of Heaven that are inaccessible even to angels.

On Friday afternoon, Rebbe Tzvi Hirsch entered the *beis midrash* before the Rizhiner, put on his *tallis*, and began leading the Minchah service, crying out loudly, "*Hodu LaHashem ki tov*" (Psalm 107).

The Rizhiner's sons felt this was chutzpah, because no one had asked him to lead the service. The Rizhiner said, "Be careful not to say anything critical about so holy a person. The *kedushah* of Shabbos burns within him with a holy passion, and it overwhelms him."

☞ Rebbe Tzvi Hirsch had yet another daughter by his third wife, and the Rebbe of Rizhin proposed that she marry his grandson. The humble tailor's apprentice was to enter into a relationship with the royalty of Chassidism! At the engagement, the Rizhiner said, "It is our custom to relate our genealogy prior to an engagement. My father was the *tzaddik*, Rebbe Shalom Shachna. My grandfather was Rebbe Avraham the *Malach*. My great-grandfather was the great Maggid of Mezeritch, the successor to the Baal Shem Tov."

Rebbe Tzvi Hirsch responded quietly, "My father was a simple and poor man. I was orphaned when I was 10, and I barely remember him. I was apprenticed to a tailor, a simple and devout man. He taught me the importance of doing an honest day's work, and he told me, 'Try to repair any defects in the old, and be cautious not to spoil anything new.' That's all I have to say."

The Rizhiner remarked, "Rebbe of Rimanov, you have outdone me."

Rebbe Tzvi Hirsch became a renowned Chassidic master, with followers in the thousands. They would hand him huge sums of money, which he promptly distributed among the poor, and when he died at the age of 70, his widow was penniless.

The *Tzaddik* of Sanz, Rebbe Chaim Halberstam, used to visit Rebbe Tzvi Hirsch as a chassid. Rebbe Shimon Sofer of Cracow asked the *Tzaddik* of Sanz why he deigned to go to Rebbe Tzvi Hirsch, since the *Tzaddik* of Sanz is a much greater Torah scholar than Rebbe Tzvi Hrsch. The *Tzaddik* said that the *Beis HaMikdash* was built on Mount Moriah rather than on Mount Sinai, where the Torah was given, because Mount Moriah is the location where Isaac was prepared to offer his life for Hashem. "Rebbe Tzvi Hirsch has *mesiras nefesh* (self-sacrifice), and every day offers up his life for Hashem."

☞ The *Tzaddik* of Sanz's son, Rebbe Baruch, needed money to marry off a daughter. He asked the *Tzaddik* for help, but was told he had no money. Several days later, a wealthy chassid gave the *Tzaddik* a significant donation, which the *Tzaddik* promptly gave to a poor person who needed to marry off a daughter.

Rebbe Baruch cried, "Am I not as deserving of help as he?"

The *Tzaddik* answered, "If you tell people that you are the son of the Rav, they will help you, but who will pay heed to this poor man if I don't?"

The *Tzaddik* continued, "I spent time with Rebbe Tzvi Hirsch of Rimanov to learn how to give *tzeddakah*. However, I was not able to achieve his level. When Rebbe Tzvi Hirsch gave away everything and had nothing left for himself, he had great *simchah*, but when I do not have any more to give away, I am in anguish."

Rebbe Tzvi Hirsch did not leave an estate, but he enriched us with the inspiration of the heights that can be reached if only one sets his mind to it.

--- *Teachings* ---

☞ The Gaon R' Meir Eizenstator, author of *Imre Aish*, met with Rebbe Tzvi Hirsch and said, "They say about you that you have *ruach hakodesh*. How can that be? The Talmud says that with the destruction of the *Beis HaMikdash* there was no longer any *ruach hakodesh*."

Rebbe Tzvi Hirsch said, "I'm surprised that you should say that. The Talmud says that with the destruction of the *Beis HaMikdash* there was no longer any *prophesying* [*Bava Basra* 12b]. Do you call what I have *ruach hakodesh?*

"Do you think that Hashem created man with eyes to see *gashmiyus* [material things] or ears to hear *gashmiyus*? A person was given eyes to see visions of G-dliness and ears to hear Heavenly pronouncements, and this is not *ruach hakodesh*. Unfortunately, due to Adam's sin and a person's own sins, one's eyes and ears have lost this ability. If a person refines his *neshamah*, and sanctifies his eyes and ears to avoid seeing and hearing *gashmiyus*, the eyes can see G-dliness and hear Heavenly pronouncements, but this is not *ruach hakodesh*."

Moses said, "[Hashem is] a G-d of faithfulness and without iniquity" (*Deuteronomy* 32:4). Rebbe Tzvi Hirsch said, "The quintessence of the Torah is to know that Hashem is 'a G-d of faithfulness and without iniquity.' You may ask, 'If so, then why the whole Torah? It would have been enough to say that one verse at Sinai.' The answer is: No one can grasp this truth until one has learned and fulfilled the whole Torah."

☞ My father related that there were several people, who, believing that Rebbe Tzvi Hirsch was ignorant of Torah, decided to humiliate him publicly. They, therefore, went to a *tisch* (Chassidic gathering with the Rebbe on Shabbos or Yom Tov), and posed a question which they were certain he could not answer.

"Rebbe," they said, "there is a Midrash on the *parashah* of the *Akeidah* which refers to a statement in the Book of Ben Sirah, אָדָם דּוֹאֵג עַל אִיבּוּד דָּמָיו וְאֵינוֹ דּוֹאֵג עַל אִיבּוּד יָמָיו — 'a person worries about the loss of his money, but does not worry as much about the loss of his days.' This means that Abraham would have been more worried about losing money than about losing his son. How can the Midrash say that about Abraham?"

Rebbe Tzvi Hirsch said, "Had you *davened* this morning, you would have known what the Midrash means.

"In the *davening*, we read the laws of the *korbanos* [sacrificial offerings]. The *korban olah* requires that its blood be applied on two corners of the Altar, to reach its four sides. The *korban bechor* (firstborn) requires only one application of its blood. If the *Kohen* does not make the proper applications of the blood, the *korban* is rendered *pasul* [unfit].

"Abraham was in a quandary. Hashem had told him to bring Isaac as an *olah* offering [*Genesis* 22:2]. However, Isaac was a firstborn to Sarah, hence, he was a *bechor*. The blood applications of an *olah* and a *bechor* are different, and if the wrong applications are made, the offering is *pasul*. Was he to consider Isaac an *olah* or a *bechor*?

"You did not translate the quotation from Ben Sirah properly. דָּמָיו does not mean 'his money.' דָּם means 'blood.' The statement means that a person (Abraham) worried about the loss of *his blood*, i.e., he was worried that the blood applications of the *korban* might be wrong, but did not worry as much about the loss of his days, because if Hashem wanted him to sacrifice Isaac, he accepted that unquestioningly."

The troublemakers' scheme had turned against them, and they left with their heads bowed in shame.

The Torah says, "These are the offspring of Noah: Noah was a *tzaddik*, a righteous man, perfect in his generations" (*Genesis* 6:9). Then it says, "Noah had begotten three sons, Shem, Ham, and Japheth." The Torah had already stated that Noah begot three sons, Shem, Ham, and Japheth (ibid. 5:32). Why the repetition?

After the Torah tells us that Noah was a *tzaddik*, it goes on to describe three types of *tzaddikim*. One is characterized by שֵׁם — name. Shem's name as a servant of Hashem goes far and wide. Another type of *tzaddik* is characterized by חָם — warmth; i.e., he may not have achieved great renown, but he serves Hashem with a burning passion. The third type of *tzaddik* does not exhibit anything extraordinary, but he is constantly close to Hashem because of his exemplary *middos*, and that is יְפֵת — beauty.

Hashem created a person with seven portals: two eyes, two ears, two nostrils, and a mouth. One must always be on guard not to look at anything forbidden, not to speak or hear what is forbidden, and not to speak angrily, not to smell (sense) anything that the Torah forbade. A person must be like a law enforcer who castigates wrongdoers and compels them to abide by the law. This is what the Torah means, "Appoint for yourself judges and officers at all your gates" (*Deuteronomy* 16:18). The gates are the seven portals, and a person is obligated to make proper judgments and enforcements so that nothing forbidden enters through these gates.

The *Targum Yerushalmi* comments on the verse, "In the beginning, Hashem created the heaven and the earth" (*Genesis* 1:1): Hashem created the world with *chachmah* (wisdom). What is wisdom? *Job* 28:28 states, "Behold! Fear of Hashem is wisdom." This is what King David referred to, saying, "How abundant are Your works, Hashem, with *chachmah* You have made them all" (*Psalms* 104:24), and King Solomon said, "She opens her mouth with *chachmah*, and the Torah of *chesed* is on her tongue (*Proverbs* 31:26).

Chachmah refers to the wisdom of truth, and the wisdom of truth is *yiras Shamayim*. This, then, leads to the conclusion of the verse in *Proverbs*: Even if a person is not learned, if he opens his mouth with the *chachmah* of *yiras Shamayim*, he will receive words of Torah as a *chesed*.

As noted, Rebbe Tzvi Hirsch was at first not considered to be a Torah scholar. This statement by Rebbe Tzvi Hirsch may be seen in that light. In his profound humility, he was saying that what he knows of Torah was given to him as a chesed of Hashem, rather than having been achieved by his own efforts.

☞ A woman, crying bitterly, came to Rebbe Tzvi Hirsch. She had been a litigant in a *din Torah* (a halachic trial) in Lemberg at the *beis din* of the *gaon* Rav Yosef Shaul Natanson (author of the *Shoel U'meishiv* responsa). The *din Torah* concerned a dispute with the heirs of her husband's estate, and the verdict had gone against her.

Rebbe Tzvi Hirsch told her to return to the *beis din* and tell the *dayanim* (judges) that they should review their sources, because they had erred.

The *dayanim* were reluctant to do so, but the woman persisted, and they found that they had indeed erred.

Some time later, Rav Yosef Shaul met Rebbe Tzvi Hirsch and asked how he could have known that they had erred, since he was not privy to their deliberations. Rebbe Tzvi Hirsch said, "*Tehillim* states, 'The laws of Hashem are upright, gladdening the soul' [*Psalms* 19:9]. When I saw the intensity of this woman's grief, I knew that there must have been an error."

The Torah says that Hashem said to Moses, "Take a census of the sons of Gershon" (*Numbers* 4:22). This is an idiomatic translation. The literal translation is, "Lift the heads of the sons of Gershon." Rebbe Tzvi Hirsch said, "'Gershon' is a derivative of the verb 'to chase away.' Hashem was telling Moses, 'Lift the heads of those people who feel that they have been separated, chased away from Hashem. Lift their spirits so that they can feel close to Hashem.'"

> *This may have been a personal response, a feeling that he had been denied closeness to Hashem because of his humble background and early paucity of learning.*

Moses said, "Eat it [the manna] today, for today is a Sabbath day for Hashem" (*Exodus* 16:25).

Rebbe Tzvi Hirsch said this verse also means, "Eat the Shabbos itself. Just as you eat the manna, you digest and absorb it, so you should take the Shabbos into yourselves as if you were eating it. Digest it and absorb it, because you will be absorbing Hashem's holy day."

The Torah says, "From there you will seek Hashem, your G-d, and you will find Him if you will search for Him with all your heart and all your soul" (*Deuteronomy* 4:29).

Rebbe Tzvi Hirsch said, "The verse also says, 'If you will seek Hashem, then you will understand that you can find Him in your heart and in your soul.'"

> *This concept is found in both Chassidic and mussar writings. Some people think that they have to look for Hashem elsewhere. In our time, there is the misconception that one must go to the Far East to find G-d. This is not true. Hashem is everywhere, near us and within us. We only must be sincere in looking for Him.*

Rebbe Tzvi Hisch said, "When the festivals, Rosh Hashanah, Yom

Kippur, and Succos are over, one is confronted with the oncoming winter months, like a person who is in a dark forest and cannot see his way, but he sees a light in the distance and heads toward it. Similarly, after Succos we head for the lights of Chanukah."

In the *parashah* of the *Akeidah*, an angel calls to Abraham and tells him not to harm Isaac, saying, "Now I know that you are one who fears G-d (*Elokim*)." Abraham then sees the ram and brings it as an offering.

An angel calls to him a second time, saying "'By Myself, I swear' — *the word of Hashem* — 'that because you ... have not withheld your son, your only one, I will surely bless you.'"

Rebbe Tzvi Hirsch asked, "Why did the first angel not give Abraham the blessing? Furthermore, the first angel referred to G-d as *Elokim*, whereas the second angel used the Name *Hashem*. Why the difference?"

Rebbe Tzvi Hirsch cited the Midrash that when Abraham was on the way to the *Akeidah*, Satan tried to discourage him, telling him that he must have misheard, because G-d would never ask for a human offering. When he saw that Abraham paid him no heed, Satan tried to convince Isaac to resist. When that failed, Satan made a deep river to block Abraham's progress, and when Abraham waded into the river up to his nose, Hashem removed the river.

When Abraham heard the angel telling him not to harm Isaac, and he saw the ram, he thought that perhaps these were more of Satan's machinations to keep him from carrying out Hashem's will. It is said that Satan has no right to pronounce the Name of Hashem, but the first angel did not use the Name of Hashem. Rather, he had said "*Elokim*," which is sometimes used to refer to judges (*Exodus* 22:7). It was only after the second angel said, "'By Myself, I swear,' — *the word of Hashem*, using the name Hashem, that Abraham was assured that it was indeed an angel of G-d and not Satan speaking to him."

☞ A man complained to Rebbe Tzvi Hirsch that he was having difficulty with *parnassah*. He had several children, and he was concerned that his difficulties would increase if his family size would increase. Therefore, he asked for a *berachah* that his wife should not bear more children. Rebbe Tzvi Hirsch told him that from the Talmud (*Yevamos* 67a) it is evident that *parnassah* comes in the merit of the children, and what he was requesting was by no means a *berachah*.

> *The Steipler Gaon responded to a similar request by stating that the amount of worry that a person will have is predestined on Rosh Hashanah. If a person tries to avoid parnassah worries by having only one or two children, he will have the same amount of worry with those one or two children as he would have had with 12 children.*

☞ On the *yahrzeit* of Rebbe Menachem Mendel, some chassidim asked Rebbe Tzvi Hirsch for money to buy *tikkun* (whiskey and cake upon which to make a *l'chaim*). Rebbe Tzvi Hirsch asked them if they had learned Mishnayos for Rebbe Menachem Mendel's *neshamah*. The chassidim said that they felt that the Rebbe's *neshamah* hardly needs their Mishnayos.

Rebbe Tzvi Hirsch said that one can observe that fish in a

stream come to the surface to catch raindrops. But why do they do that? They are fully immersed in a great deal of water. Obviously, even though they have abundant water, they want every drop of fresh water they can get.

Similarly, the *neshamos* of *tzaddikim* have abundant *zechusim*. Nevertheless, they appreciate every additional *zechus* they can receive.

The Torah states that the angels left Abraham to go to Sodom, "while Abraham was still standing before Hashem" (*Genesis* 18:22).

Rebbe Tzvi Hirsch points out that the verb in this verse is in the present tense, and an accurate translation is, "and Abraham *is still standing* before Hashem." The Torah is telling us that *Avraham Avinu*, even today, stands before Hashem to pray for his children.

"If you hearken diligently to the voice of Hashem, and do what is just in His eyes, give ear to His commandments and observe all His decrees, then any of the diseases that I placed upon Egypt, I will not bring upon you, for I am Hashem your Healer" (*Exodus* 15:26).

Rebbe Tzvi Hirsch commented, "If they will not have the diseases, what need is there for healing?"

It is known that Rambam was the sultan's court physician. One day the sultan asked, "How do I know that you are a good doctor? I have never needed your treatment, because I have never been ill."

Rambam answered, "That is precisely the test of a good physician: to prescribe a health regimen that will prevent his client from becoming sick."

This is what Hashem is saying. "Because I am your Healer, I will see that you should not suffer the diseases inflicted upon the

Egyptians."

On the opening verse of the Torah, Rashi cites a Midrashic statement by R' Yitzchak, stating that the Torah should have begun with the first mitzvah the Jews were given: הַחֹדֶשׁ הַזֶּה לָכֶם. What is the reason the Torah begins with the account of Creation? So that all nations should know that the world belongs to Hashem, He created it, and He can give any land to whomever He wishes.

Rebbe Tzvi Hirsch said that there is another way to read R' Yitzchak's statement. וּמַה טַעַם פָּתַח בִּבְרֵאשִׁית is not necessarily a question, but rather an exclamation. "מַה טַעַם פָּתַח בִּבְרֵאשִׁית! — How sweet a taste it is that Hashem told us the account of Creation!"

In the Chanukah prayer we say that "the Greek kingdom rose up against Your people to make them forget Your Torah and compel them to stray from the statutes of Your will."

Rebbe Tzvi Hirsch interprets the last phrase to mean that not only did they want to suppress observance of the Torah, but they wanted to "brainwash" the Jews so that they should not even have the *will* to observe Torah.

> *The aphorism, "There is nothing that stands in the way of the will," is generally assumed to be of Talmudic origin. Actually, this is not found anywhere in Talmud and is a paraphrase of Zohar (162:2). This is not the same as the popular "Where there is a will, there is a way." Obviously, there are many things that a person may want but cannot get. However, although one may not be able to get everything one wants, there is nothing to stop someone from wanting something. The concept that the Zohar states is that at least one should*

want to do what is right. Sometimes circumstances may preclude a person's doing a particular mitzvah, but no circumstances should preclude one from wanting to do a mitzvah.

Rebbe Tzvi Hirsch used to tell the people who came to spend time with him that it is not sufficient that they are very spiritual in his presence. They must maintain this status even after they leave him. He pointed to the spies, of whom the Torah says that they were great men, but that was only in the presence of Moses. Once they left Moses, they suffered a sharp descent, resulting in our national tragedy.

Stories

The Rav of Barniva, who was a grandson of Rebbe Eliezer of Dzhikov, told the following story.

"Almost 10 years after his marriage, my father, who was Rav of Barniva before me, had not been blessed with a child. He told his wife that if after 10 years they did not have a child, the Shulchan Aruch says that he may divorce her. When my father heard that Rebbe Tzvi Hirsch was coming to Dzhikov, he went to see him. Rebbe Tzvi Hirsch would collect money for the local poor and also sent huge amounts to support the community in Eretz Yisrael. He would, therefore, ask for large contributions.

"My mother was able to get an appointment to see Rebbe Tzvi Hirsch, and she burst out crying, that her husband said he would divorce her if she did not have a child soon. "I don't want any other husband. My husband is a *tzaddik* and my father-in-law is a *tzaddik*. How much money does the Rebbe want for a *berachah* that I should have a child?"

Rebbe Tzvi Hirsch said, "Should I ask for money from the daughter-in-law of the Rebbe of Dzhikov?" but my mother carried on, and Rebbe Tzvi Hirsch finally said, "If you give me 150 reinish for *tzeddakah*, I will give you a *berachah* for a son."

My mother told this to my father. They simply did not possess anywhere near 150 reinish, and they consulted the Rebbe of Dzhikov, who said, "Don't hesitate for a moment. Take your wedding headpiece which is embroidered with pearls, and give it to Rebbe Tzvi Hirsch as a pledge."

Rebbe Tzvi Hirsch accepted the pledge and said to my mother, "Bow your head and I will bless you," It was his custom to raise his hands and pronounce the priestly blessing. This time, he held his hands above my mother's hands in silence, then said, "You are already conceived of a son. May Hashem bless you that you carry out your pregnancy and have a healthy child."

The Rebbe of Dzhikov said, "We knew that Rebbe Tzvi Hirsch's *berachos* are powerful, but that he could know that a woman had conceived before she was aware of it, that we did not know." He told his sons to observe how Rebbe Tzvi Hirsch steps back after completing the *Amidah* prayer, because "then you will know what it means for a person to totally efface oneself before Hashem."

When Rebbe Tzvi Hirsch *davened*, the Rebbe of Dzhikov could not tear his eyes off him. He said to his father, Rebbe Naftali of Ropshitz, "I saw the Heavenly angels dancing beside him."

Rebbe Naftali said, "Yes, I saw that, too."

Before Rebbe Tzvi Hirsch left Dzhikov, he said, "Let me know when the child is born. I want to be the *Kohen* at the *pidyon haben*. The five shekalim I receive are kosher money that Hashem has awarded me as a *Kohen*."

The Rav of Barniva said, "My father felt privileged that he came into the world with a *berachah* from Rebbe Tzvi Hirsch. Unfortunately, he did not have the privilege of having him as a *Kohen* at his *pidyon haben*, because in the interim Rebbe Tzvi Hirsch died."

A woman came to Rebbe Tzvi Hirsch for a *berachah,* and he lifted his hands above her head to bless her. "Why doesn't the Rebbe put his hands on my head?" she asked.

Rebbe Tzvi Hirsch said, "When you light the Shabbos candles, why do you put your hands above the candles rather than directly on them?"

The woman said, "I don't want to get burned."

Rebbe Tzvi Hirsch said, "So it is with me."

After Rebbe Tzvi Hirsch's wife died, a woman came to ask for a *berachah* that she find a proper husband. Rebbe Tzvi Hirsch asked her where she was from, who her family was, and who her parents were.

After she had answered his questions, Rebbe Tzvi Hirsch said, "I can suggest a *shidduch* for you: myself."

The woman was stunned, but after she regained her composure, she said, "If it pleases the Rebbe, I am willing."

Rebbe Tzvi Hirsch asked his *gabbai* to bring in cake and something to drink and invited several people. He told them, "When I was an apprentice to a tailor, I used to run errands, bringing him material and delivering the finished garments. There was one house to which I delivered items a number of times on Friday morning. It was a large family with many children, and I would deliver the children's Shabbos clothes that the tailor had repaired. When I came into the house, the table was set for Shabbos, the candlesticks, the challos, and the wine all were on the table. The man of the house was sitting at the table, reviewing the *parashah* of the week. Some people did not pay immediately, but this man promptly paid, and when he gave me the money he would say, 'I hereby fulfill the mitzvah of "On that day you shall pay his hire"'(*Deuteronomy* 24:15).

"I looked forward to coming to that house on Friday morning, because I could feel it permeated with the *kedushah* of Shabbos. I once said to myself, I wish I could become a member of that family. The woman I am to wed is a daughter of that man."

"I am grateful to Hashem that He has made my wish a reality."

Rebbe Yaakov Yitzchak HaLevi Horowitz
the Chozeh ("Seer") of Lublin (1747-1815)

There are stories about how the parents of *tzaddikim* merited having such special children. This story, however, is not about the *Chozeh's* father, but about his grandfather, Reb Koppel of Likuv.

↝ Reb Koppel earned his livelihood by brewing beer and whiskey, which he then sold in his inn. Before Passover, he would sell his inventory to a non-Jew. One year, the priest of Likuv, who was an ardent anti-Semite, issued a decree forbidding any of the townspeople to buy the *chametz* from Reb Koppel. On the day before Passover, when Reb Koppel could find no one to buy the *chametz*, he moved all the barrels of beer and whiskey outdoors, declared them to be *hefker* (i.e., he abandoned ownership of them), and informed the townsfolk that they could help themselves to the beer and whiskey. He then took his family to spend Passover in a nearby village with relatives.

When he returned to the town after Passover, the townsfolk greeted him derisively. "So, you tell us to help ourselves to the beer and whiskey; then you put vicious dogs to guard it!" Reb Koppel didn't have a clue as to what they meant. When he reached his house, he saw two huge dogs standing near the barrels of beer and whiskey. When the dogs saw Reb Koppel, they quietly slunk away.

Reb Koppel consulted his Rebbe. It is forbidden to have *chametz* in one's possession on Passover, and one must make it *hefker*, allowing anyone to take it. But no one could take his *chametz* because it was guarded by dogs. It is forbidden to have any benefit from *chametz* that was not disposed of before Passover. Was he permitted to sell the beer and whiskey?

The Rebbe said that he had properly disposed of the *chametz* by making it *hefker* and placing it outside, where anyone could take it. Because of his devotion to Hashem and his *mesiras nefesh* in disposing of the *chametz*, Hashem had rewarded him by having dogs guard it. Therefore, he was permitted to make use of the beer and whiskey. However, Reb Koppel discarded the beer and whiskey, saying it was not to one's benefit to profit from a miracle (see *Taanis* 24b).

For his *mesiras nefesh,* Reb Koppel was rewarded with a grandchild who became the *Chozeh* of Lublin.

An additional story is related about Reb Koppel.

- Reb Koppel rented his property from a *poritz*. His inn was always open to travelers, and Reb Koppel fulfilled the mitzvah of *hachnasas orchim* (hospitality to wayfarers) and *tzeddakah* in a superlative way. Some local anti-Semites were envious and told the *poritz* that the income from the inn could not suffice to cover his lavish expenditures. Obviously, Reb Koppel must be acting illegally to have made so much money.

Although the *poritz* believed Reb Koppel to be an honest person, the repetitive accusations raised his suspicions. One day he came to the inn, and Reb Koppel greeted him warmly,

The *poritz* said, "I understand that you give much money to charity and that you feed many wayfarers who are unable to pay. Where do you get all that money?"

"Come with me to the cellar," Reb Koppel said, "and I will show you." After they had descended to the cellar, Reb Koppel filled a container with alcohol and gave the *poritz* an instrument to measure the strength of the alcohol. The *poritz* said, "This is pure spirits, 100 percent alcohol."

Reb Koppel emptied half the container and filled it with water. "Measure it now," he said.

The *poritz* was astounded. "Why, it is pure spirits, 100 percent alcohol! I don't understand."

Reb Koppel said, "My G-d wants me to give charity and food to the needy. This is how He provides for me."

The *poritz* said, "I always thought you to be an honest person, but I never knew that you were an angel of G-d."

☞ One Friday, Rep Koppel was traveling to town to buy provisions for Shabbos, and he came across a poor, shabbily dressed man walking down the road. "Come up into the wagon," he said.

"No, I prefer to walk," the man said.

"Why should you walk when you can ride?" Reb Koppel asked.

The man said, "I know your kind. You don't really care whether I am tired or not. You are just trying to do a mitzvah to be rewarded. Well, I don't want you to use me for your selfish purposes."

Reb Koppel said, "I will give you the reward of this mitzvah. Just come into the wagon."

"If you are sincere about giving away the reward for the mitzvah, let's make it a binding transaction with a handshake," the man said.

After Reb Koppel shook the man's hand, the latter said, "Now I can reveal myself to you. I am the Angel of Death, and I was told to take your *neshamah*. The Heavenly angels protested to Hashem, saying, 'The Torah says that *tzeddakah* rescues from death [*Proverbs* 10:2]. Reb Koppel has given so much *tzeddakah*. Is it fair that he should die so young?'

"I told them," the Angel of Death said, "that the Torah is not referring to someone who gives *tzeddakah* in order to earn reward, but only to someone who sincerely cares for others and not for himself."

"Hashem then said, 'Go down and test Reb Koppel and satisfy yourself whether his *tzeddakah* is sincere or not.' Since you were willing to give away your reward, I will grant you 25 more years of life. You will live to marry off not only your daughter, but also the son that she will bear."

That son was the *Chozeh*.

Rebbe Yaakov Yitzchak acquired the appellation *Chozeh* because of his prophetic vision. It is related that in his youth he wore headgear that restricted his peripheral vision to prevent him from seeing anything indecent. His eyes were focused on the ground beneath him, so that he would not see anything beyond four cubits. It is said that because his eyes never saw anything improper, he developed prophetic vision. Perhaps this was the reason that Rebbe Elimelech bequeathed him his power of vision.

As a young man, Rebbe Yaakov Yitzchak was an accomplished Torah scholar. He entered into a Torah discussion with a young man who was also well learned in Talmud, but who was very lax in Torah observance. Realizing that knowledge of Torah was not enough to protect a person from deviating from it, Rebbe Yaakov Yitzchak went to shul, opened the *Aron Kodesh* (ark) and prayed tearfully that Hashem should show him the way of truth.

After prolonged prayer, a man of saintly but awesome appearance said to him, "If you are seeking truth, go to Rovna."

"Who are you?" Rebbe Yaakov Yitzchak asked.

"My name is Avraham," the man said, and disappeared.

The Maggid of Mezeritch was then in Rovna, and at the Maggid's home, Rebbe Yaakov Yitzchak met his disciples. It is said that before he came, the Maggid told his disciples, "Coming to visit us is a *neshamah* that has not been sent to earth since the days of the prophets." Rebbe Yaakov Yitzchak continued his visits to the Maggid, but ultimately became a disciple of Rebbe Elimelech.

☞ The *Chozeh* had the habit of doing something minor to help in preparing his food for Shabbos. One Friday in Mezeritch, he went into the kitchen and and salted a slice of fish. Rebbe Shneur Zalman of Liadi wondered how the *Chozeh* could know that he would be served that specific piece. Reb Shneur Zalman marked the portion with an identifying thread.

At the Friday-night meal, this piece of fish was offered to the person seated next to the *Chozeh*, but as he reached for it, his hands began to tremble, and the fish was passed to the *Chozeh*. Rebbe Shneur Zalman then realized the *Chozeh's* greatness.

☞ The *Chozeh* studied Torah in Ritchval under the great gaon, Rebbe Shmelke, who was later Rabbi of Nikolsburg. Every day, the *Chozeh* recited the morning *berachos* for Rebbe Shmelke, who responded with "Amen." Rebbe Shmelke saw that the other students were envious of the *Chozeh*, and said to them, "When Yaakov Yitzchak says a *berachah*, the heavenly angels answer 'Amen.'"

One of the *Chozeh's chaverim* (peers) at Rebbe Shmelke's yeshivah said, "Yaakov Yitzchak would sit in an inconspicuous place. He never asked questions like the rest. He never looked at any of us, only at the Rebbe. When he was not looking into a *sefer,* he kept his eyes lowered."

Although Rebbe Shmelke himself had a tendency to aloofness, he felt that Yaakov Yitzchak's attitude was excessive. He sent him to Rebbe Zusia of Anipole with a note, "Make our Itzikel a little lighter of heart."

☞ After Rebbe Shmelke's death, the *Chozeh* became a devoted disciple of Rebbe Elimelech of Lizhensk. Several of Rebbe Elimelech's senior disciples were engaged in a halachic discussion while awaiting Rebbe Elimelech's entrance. The *Chozeh*, who was a newcomer to Lizhensk, said to them, "Discussing halachah in the Rebbe's absence is disrespectful," and the group fell silent.

Rebbe Naftali of Ropschitz was still a very young man and was stunned by the *Chozeh's* boldness in challenging the older disciples. As the *Chozeh* left, Rebbe Naftali followed him to his coach and said, "Rebbe, give me a *berachah*!"

"Go away," the *Chozeh* said. "Don't call me 'Rebbe.' The only Rebbe is the master. I'm not a Rebbe and I don't give *berachos*."

Rebbe Naftali said, "I am shivering out here in the cold, but I won't leave until you give me a *berachah*."

The *Chozeh* blessed him, and years later said, "Ropchick [that is how he affectionately referred to Rebbe Naftali] manipulated me and received the first *berachah* I ever gave."

The *Chozeh* was extremely humble. Before studying Torah, he would tearfully say, *"Ribono shel Olam*, how dare I learn Torah? Perhaps I am the one of whom it is said, 'And to the *rasha* Hashem said, "Why do you speak My laws, and carry My covenant on your mouth?"' [*Psalms* 50:16]. Please, Hashem, I know I've been sinful, but that was in the past. I promise that from now on I'll be good. Yes, I promised that yesterday and did not fulfill it, but this time I'm sincere, and I'll fulfill my promise to be good."

☞ When the *Chozeh* was returning from the *tashlich* ritual (figuratively casting one's sins into the river), he met Rebbe Naftali of Ropschitz heading toward the water. "Where are you going?" the *Chozeh* asked.

Rebbe Naftali replied, "I am going to retrieve the sins that the Rebbe threw away. What the Rebbe considers sins are mitzvos for me."

The *Chozeh's yiras shamayim* was such that he trembled during *tefillah*. When the *Tzaddik* of Sanz spoke of the intensity of the *Chozeh's avodas Hashem*, a chassid said to him, "What could be greater than the Rebbe's *avodas Hashem*?" The *tzaddik* replied, "Had you seen the *avodas Hashem* of the *Chozeh* you would dismiss my *avodas Hashem* as being nothing."

The *Tzaddik* of Apta said that the *Chozeh* was so totally devoted to *avodas Hashem* that he did not make a move without it being in the interest of *avodas Hashem*. "Indeed, he does not even raise his eyelids without intention of *avodas Hashem*."

☞ On one occasion that the *Chozeh* visited the Baal Shem Tov's grandson, Rebbe Baruch of Medzhibozh. Rebbe Baruch was going to immerse in the river (as a *mikveh*), and the *Chozeh* accompanied him.

At one point, Rebbe Baruch asked, "Where does the Rebbe from Poland sense that we are?"

The *Chozeh* said, "I sense the *kedushah* of Eretz Yisrael."

A bit later, Rebbe Baruch asked, "And now?"

The *Chozeh* said, "The *kedushah* of Jerusalem."

A bit later, Rebbe Baruch asked, "And now?"

"The Holy of Holies," the *Chozeh* said.

When they had immersed in the river, Rabbi Baruch said, "And what does the Rebbe from Poland sense now?'

The *Chozeh* said. "The pure, fragrant river of *Gan Eden*."

Rebbe Baruch said, "Yes, it is true what they say of you. You are a true *chozeh*."

☞ When the *Tzaddik* of Sanz, Rebbe Chaim Halberstam, was

a youngster, he was recognized as an *ilui* (a child prodigy in Torah). His father, Reb Leibish of Tarnograd, was a merchant who did not think well of chassidim. When young Chaim told his father that he wanted to see the Rebbe of Lublin, his father objected, because he feared that it would distract the boy from his Torah study. When Chaim persisted, Reb Leibish yielded and took him to Lublin.

The *Chozeh* welcomed young Chaim warmly. "Do you know much Torah?" he asked.

The boy answered. "I try my best to learn."

The *Chozeh* said, "There is a *Tosafos* [Talmudic commentary] that is difficult to understand. Perhaps you can resolve this difficulty."

Young Chaim retired to the *beis midrash* and discussed the problematic *Tosafos* with some of the scholars, but no one could resolve the difficulty. The boy then studied the *gemara* for several hours and felt that he had resolved the problem. He told the *Chozeh* his understanding of the *Tosafos*, and the *Chozeh* was thrilled with young Chaim's genius.

The *Chozeh* then asked everyone to leave the room, and when he was alone with Chaim, he said to him, "*Yiddele*, you will one day be a leader of Israel. People will come to you with *kvitlach*. Let me show you how you are to read a *kvitel*."

The *Chozeh* paced to and fro, mumbling to himself. Then he said to the young Chaim, "*Yiddele*, when we had the *Beis HaMikdash*, the *Kohen Gadol* [high priest] wore the *Urim VeTumim* in his breastplate, and Hashem made His will known via the *Urim VeTumim*. Now that we have no *Beis HaMikdash* and no *Urim*

VeTumim, we can see the light of Hashem's Name in the Torah. People come to me with their problems and requests for *berachos*, and over a period of time, I felt that the transmitted light of Hashem had become attenuated. I needed to replenish it, so I studied the mishnah of *Eizehu mekomon* [*Zevachim, Perek* 5] to renew the light of Torah. *Yiddele*, remember this when you become a leader in Israel. Your only strength and your only wisdom are through Torah."

☞ Many great Torah personalities attested to the greatness of the *Chozeh*. Rebbe Yekusiel Yehudah Teitelbaum (author of *Yetev Lev*) related that his grandfather, Rebbe Moshe Teitelbaum (author of *Yismach Moshe*), had no interest in chassidim or rebbes. However, his son-in-law, author of *Aryeh D'Bei Ilaa*, who was an outstanding Torah scholar and an adherent of the *Chozeh*, urged the *Yismach Moshe* to visit the *Chozeh*.

Knowing that the *Yismach Moshe* was planning a trip to Lublin, someone asked him to take a silver snuffbox to the *Chozeh*. He recalled that the Talmud says that if one brings a gift to a *talmid chacham* it is as though he brought the offering of *bikkurim* (first-ripened fruits) to the Sanctuary (*Kesubos* 105b). The *Yismach Moshe* reflected, "The Talmud does not say, 'one who *gives* a gift to a *talmid chacham*' or 'one who sends a gift,' but rather, 'one who *brings* a gift to a *talmid chacham*.'"

En route he thought, "How can chassidim justify their joyfulness when the Shulchan Aruch says that a G-d-fearing person should mourn the loss of the *Beis HaMikdash*?" Then he thought, "Perhaps the *tzaddik* of Lublin can clarify that for me. After all, the Sages said, 'If a person desires to become pure, they will assist him' (*Shabbos* 104a). The Talmud does not say, *He* [Hashem] will assist him, but rather *they* will assist him,' which must mean that *talmidei chachamim* will assist him."

When the *Yismach Moshe* met the *Chozeh,* he was warmly greeted. "*Shalom aleichem*, Rav of Shinova," the *Chozeh* said. (The *Yismach Moshe* was Rav in Shinova before Uheli.) "Why do you seem so morose? True, the Shulchan Aruch says that we should mourn the loss of the *Beis HaMikdash,* but the *Chovos HaLevavos* says that one should mourn in his heart, but one's face should be cheerful. When we say *tikun chatzos* [midnight lamentations for the *Beis HaMikdash*], we grieve and cry bitterly.

"My great teacher, Rebbe Shmelke of Nikolsburg, related that a king was driven from his throne, and found refuge in the house of one of his subjects. The latter, seeing the king's plight, was deeply saddened, yet was happy that he had the privilege of hosting his king. So it is with us. We grieve that the *Shechinah* was driven from its place, but we rejoice that it has found a place to rest with us.

"You see, Rav of Shinova, the Talmud says that if a person desires to become pure, 'they will assist him.' Note that it does not say *He* will assist him, but rather *they* will assist him."

When the *Yismach Moshe* gave the *Chozeh* the silver snuffbox, the latter opened it and said, "Why, this has the fragrance of *bikkurim*! Did you note, Rav of Shinova, that the Talmud does not say 'one who gives a gift to a *talmid chacham*' or 'one who sends a gift,' but rather, 'one who *brings* a gift'?"

The *Yismach Moshe* was stunned by the *Chozeh's ruach hakodesh* and became a devoted follower.

☞ That Shabbos, the *Yismach Moshe* remained in Lublin and *davened* together with the *Chozeh*. He was *davening* with great *kavannah* when he suddenly remembered that he left the key to the strongbox in the lock, and *tzeddakah* money for orphans was there. This disturbed his concentration for several minutes, but he was able to set it aside and return to his *kavannah*.

At the morning meal, the *Chozeh* said to the *Yismach Moshe*, "What happened to you, Rav of Shinova? Until *Nishmas* you were together with me, then I lost you until the *berachah* of *Yotzer Ohr*. So, if one forgot a key, is that any reason to be distracted from one's *kavannah*?"

The *Chozeh* had many disciples, all of whom were great Torah luminaries, and all of whom refer to the *Chozeh* in glowing, superlative terms. Among them are Rebbe Zvi Elimelech of Dinov (author of *Bnei Yisasschar*), Rebbe Yaakov Yitzchak of Pshische (the *Yehudi HaKadosh*), Rebbe Simchah Bunim of Pshische, Rebbe Naftali of Ropschitz, Rebbe Yechezkel of Kuzmir, Rebbe Meir HaLevi of Apta, Rebbe David of Lelov, Rebbe Shalom of Belz, Rebbe Shimon of Yaraslov, and Rebbe Klonimus Kalman (author of *Maor VaShemesh*). It is said that the *Chozeh* assembled 400 disciples, and that the sight of them on a Shabbos, all dressed in white kaftans, was like a vision of angels.

☞ The *Chozeh* delegated two people to go to Tomashav and inform Mendel that he should come to the *Chozeh*. The two met many Mendels in Tomashav, but they did not feel that anyone of them was the person the *Chozeh* intended. They slept on benches in the *beis midrash* (study hall that was also used as a shul), and at midnight, they saw a young man come in, recite *Tehillim* (*Psalms*) with heartrending tears, and then open the Aron Kodesh, saying, "Master of the Universe! Show me even just an iota of truth."

The two men said to him, "If you are looking for truth, come with us to Lublin."

Mendel came to Lublin on Friday morning, and bought a small pocketknife to cut his nails before going to the *mikveh*. After the *mikveh* he went to see the *Chozeh*, who said, "Young man, is that why you came to Lublin, to buy a pocketknife?"

Mendel said, "You are not going to attract me with a show of *ruach hakodesh*. I came to find truth." Mendel remained in Lublin, and subsequently became a follower of two of the *Chozeh's* disciples, the *Yehudi HaKadosh* and Rebbe Simchah Bunim of Pshische. He later gained renown as the Rebbe of Kotzk, who was a fierce champion of truth.

The *Chozeh* said, "I prefer a *rasha* who knows that he is a *rasha* to a *tzaddik* who knows he is a *tzaddik*. Why? Because the *rasha* knows the truth, whereas anyone who thinks he is a *tzaddik* deceives himself."

In keeping with the Baal Shem Tov's teaching, the *Chozeh* stressed maintaining *simchah* under all circumstances.

☞ The *Chozeh* once visited the Rav of Ostila, who was a son of the Chassidic master, Rebbe Mordechai of Neschitz. Knowing the *Chozeh's* sensitivity, the Rav had a bed constructed especially for him, and told the carpenter to go to the *mikveh* before building this bed. However, when the *Chozeh* lay down on the bed, he began to exclaim that he felt stabbing pain. The Rav was surprised, because the bed had been built with the utmost purity.

"Yes," the *Chozeh* said, "but it was put together in the three weeks of mourning before *Tishah B'Av*, and the carpenter's sadness permeated the bed."

The *Chozeh* said that a person who celebrates a *simchah* is referred to as a *baal simchah*, which means "one who possesses *simchah*," and as such, can dispense *simchah* to others. He urged people who were celebrating *simchos* to bless others with *simchah*.

☞ One of the *Chozeh's* disciples, Rebbe Dov Ber of Ropschitz, lodged at an inn. In the morning he asked the innkeeper where he had acquired his clock. "Every time the clock struck the hour, I felt an urge to get up and dance." The innkeeper said that he had been given the clock as a pledge by a guest who had no money to pay his bill.

Rebbe Dov Ber asked, "Did the guest mention anything about the *Chozeh* of Lublin?"

The innkeeper said, "Yes, he said that he was related to the *Chozeh*."

"I knew it!" Rebbe Dov Ber said. "You see, a clock is really a sad instrument. Every time it strikes the hour, it means that an hour of your life has irretrievably passed. The *Chozeh's* clock was different. Every hour was one hour closer to the coming of *Mashiach*."

The *Chozeh* once told his household that he needed to arise very early the next morning, and requested that they have the evening meal early that day. They neglected to do so, and, in fact, served the meal later than usual. The *Chozeh* said, "This is adequate reason for me to be angry at them. But my reason to get up early was to do Hashem's will, and it is Hashem's will that I should not be angry."

My father related that *Avraham Avinu* was able to be in constant contact with Hashem, but he knew that his descendants would not be able to do so. Therefore, he composed Shacharis whereby his descendants would be able to commune with Hashem. This displeased Satan, who brought alien thoughts to people so that they could not concentrate on *tefillah*.

Yitzchak Avinu said, "Perhaps it is difficult for people to maintain concentration for a lengthy period of time. I will compose a brief *tefillah*, Minchah, during which people will be able to focus their minds." But here, too, Satan was able to deflect people's thoughts.

Yaakov Avinu said, "Shacharis and Minchah are mandatory. I will compose an optional *tefillah*, Maariv, which will not draw Satan's attention." But here, too, Satan was able to interfere.

The Baal Shem Tov came up with another idea. One should engage in ordinary conversation, but concentrate on communing with Hashem. It will not occur to Satan that this ordinary conversation is a disguise for prayer.

This was a technique that we find in the Talmud, which says that Rav never uttered a word on secular matters (*Succah* 28:1). Are we to understand that the other great Talmudic Sages did speak secular talk? "Heaven forbid!" my father said. "The other *tzaddikim* either spoke in Torah or were silent. Rav developed the technique of speaking what sounded like secular talk, but his words were actually words of prayer, disguised as common speech. This is why the Talmud says, 'One should study even the conversation of Torah scholars' (*Avodah Zarah* 19b)."

☞ Every day, the *Chozeh* would say a special *tefillah* expressing his gratitude to Hashem for sending to this world a *neshamah* as holy as Rebbe Levi Yitzchak of Berditchev.

A great Torah scholar, Rav Azriel Horowitz, lived in Lublin. He was known as *Der Eizener Kop* (the Iron Head) because of his superior intellect. Rav Azriel was associated with the misnagdim, a group that opposed Chassidism, and was critical of the *Chozeh*. He once said to the *Chozeh,* "What makes you think that you are a *tzaddik*? Why do all these people come to you? You are deceiving them. Tell them not to come to you."

The *Chozeh* did as Rav Azriel suggested, and on Shabbos, he addressed all assembled, saying, "There is no reason for you to come to me. You have been deceived into thinking that I am a *tzaddik*." That only increased the number of his followers.

Rav Azriel then said, "Of course! When you said that, they thought you were being humble and that increased your stature in their eyes. Just do the opposite. Say, 'You should all come to me because I am a great *tzaddik*!'"

The *Chozeh* said, "I can't say that. I'm not a *tzaddik*, but I'm not a liar, either."

When the *Chozeh* first came to Lublin, he met strong opposition from the misnagdim, who were in the overwhelming majority, but he gradually won many of them to his side.

☞ It was the custom that early in the morning the *shamash* would go from door to door, rousing the people to come to shul on time. One of the misnagdim once saw the *shamash* approaching the *Chozeh's* house, and the *Chozeh* called to him through the window, "Stay where you are! Don't move!" A moment later, the *Chozeh* emerged with a container of water, and had the *shamash* wash his hands. It turned out that the *shamash* had been at a wedding until the wee hours of the morning, and when he awoke, he realized he had overslept. In his haste, he ran out of the house without washing his hands. The *Chozeh* had thus prevented the *shamash* from violating a law in the Shulchan Aruch, by walking further with unwashed hands. The misnaged who observed this became a follower of the *Chozeh*.

HaGaon Rav Baruch Frankl, known in the Torah world by the name of his *sefer, Baruch Taam*, had a son, Yehoshua Heschel. He had "defected" to the chassidim, much to the chagrin of his father, who was affiliated with the misnagdim. (It is interesting to note that the *Baruch Taam*'s son-in-law was Rebbe Chaim Halberstam of Sanz, one of the foremost Chassidic masters.) Yehoshua Heschel, an accomplished Torah scholar, became an ardent adherent of the *Chozeh*.

The *Chozeh* told Yehoshua Heschel that he should frequent Rav Azriel's court. Yehoshua Heschel did not understand why, but did not question the Rebbe's word. Rav Azriel welcomed Yehoshua Heschel, because, although he was a chassid, he was the son of the great *Baruch Taam*.

One day, Yehoshua Heschel was present at a *din Torah* at which

Rav Azriel presided. He heard the arguments presented by the litigants and the discussion of the *dayanim*. He was shocked that Rav Azriel's opinion did not follow halachah. He approached Rav Azriel, asking him to clarify a difficult *Tosafos* for him. Rav Azriel said he would do so after the *din Torah*, but Yehoshua Heschel insisted that he must do so immediately. When Rav Azriel studied the *Tosafos*, he realized that he had erred in his judgment, and gave the proper verdict.

The next day, the *Chozeh* told Yehoshua Heschel, "There is no longer a need for you to go to Rav Azriel."

> *After several years, Yehoshua Heschel returned to Leipnik, but was hesitant to go directly to his father. The Baruch Taam was giving a shiur in Talmud, and raised several difficult issues about a passage in the Talmud which could not be resolved. Yehoshua Heschel told one of the students that if one interpreted the passage a bit differently, the difficulties would disappear. The student related this to the Baruch Taam, who realized that this explication could not be this student's own interpretation.*
>
> *"Who told you that?" the Baruch Taam asked.*
>
> *"The young man sitting outside," the talmid replied.*
>
> *Yehoshua Heschel then went into the beis midrash and his father embraced him. He realized that his fear that his son would not become a Torah scholar if he joined the chassidim was unfounded.*

☞ The *Chozeh* was given the honor of being the *sandek* (godfather) at a *bris* in a village near Lublin. For a number of reasons, his trip was delayed, and the father of the infant decided not to keep the guests waiting any longer. The *bris* was performed and, as they were about to begin the meal that accompanies a *bris,* the *Chozeh* arrived. During the meal, the *Chozeh* was unusually jubilant. He explained, "Being a *sandek* is a great mitzvah, and one must have all the proper *kavannos* [thoughts; in this case, esoteric kabbalistic formulas]. Who can have all the proper *kavannos*? However, the Talmud says that if a person intends to do a mitzvah but circumstances beyond his control prevent him from doing it, Hashem considers it as though he did the mitzvah. Now, Hashem knows all the proper *kavannos,* so the credit I will receive is for a mitzvah that was done with all the proper *kavannos.*"

The great *gaon,* Rav Meir Yechiel of Ostrovza, reports that he read the following in the chronicles of Lublin:

> The chief rabbi of Lublin, Rav Shaul Margolis, limited formation of *shtiblach* (small, unpretentious synagogues), because he felt that the upkeep of the main synagogue required everyone's participation. The only exception made was for the *tzaddik* Rebbe Yaakov Yitzchak Horowitz (the *Chozeh*), who was permitted to have a permanent synagogue of his own, because it was evident that he was imbued with *ruach hakodesh,* as was indicated by the following episode.
>
> A man came to Lublin with a power of attorney from a wealthy man instructing him to find a *shidduch* for his daughter. Upon finding a fine young scholar from a highly reputable family, he finalized the *shidduch.* This man was an accomplished Torah scholar, a misnaged, who, hearing

much about the *Chozeh*, was curious and went to see him.

The *Chozeh* asked what had brought him to Lublin, and he answered that he was sent to find a *chasan* for the daughter of a wealthy man. "However," he said, "I would like to have a Torah discussion with you."

The *Chozeh* said, "You have certainly studied the Prophets, haven't you?"

The man thought that the *Chozeh* was belittling him and said, "Of course."

"Then let me ask you to explain the verse that appears in the text when Saul and his servant went to look for the lost donkeys. They asked where they could find the Seer [as the prophet Samuel was then called], because, 'Perhaps he can show us the way in which we have gone' [*I Samuel* 9:6]. What sense does that make? They knew the way that they had gone. What they needed to know was which way they *should* go to find the donkeys."

The man could not answer the question, and said, "Please explain the verse to me."

The *Chozeh* said, "Saul understood that inasmuch as they had not found the donkeys, that was not their purpose for being there. His question was, 'Then for what purpose did we come?' Samuel's answer was that inasmuch as the donkeys had already been found, that was not their purpose. Rather, it was to bring Saul to Samuel so that the prophet could anoint him as king of Israel.

"So, inasmuch as this *shidduch* will not materialize, for what purpose did you come to Lublin?"

These words penetrated the man's mind, and he proceeded to inquire further about the *chasan*. He discovered that there was serious question about the family's legitimacy. He dissolved the *shidduch* and paid the required fine. The man then became a devoted follower of the *Chozeh*.

One of the *Chozeh's* leading disciples was Rebbe Yaakov Yitzchak of Pshische, known in Chassidic literature as the *Yehudi HaKadosh* (the holy Jew). Some say this title was used because his name is the same as that of the *Chozeh*, and it was improper to refer to the Master's first name.

When the *Yehudi HaKadosh* first came to Lublin, the *Chozeh* greeted him jubilantly. The *Chozeh* said, "It was revealed to me that my successor would have my name. A few days ago, a man named Yaakov Yitzchak ben Devorah Meitel, exactly my name and my mother's name, came to see me. I was very upset because he is not qualified to be my successor. Now that you have come, I see that you are the designated one."

☞ A strong bond existed between the *Chozeh* and the *Yehudi HaKadosh*. The *Chozeh* once asked him, "Why do you *daven* so quickly? You seem to be swallowing the words."

The *Yehudi HaKadosh* responded, "The words are so sweet that I want to swallow them all at once."

The *Chozeh* said, "Don't you think I find the words sweet? Yet I don't swallow them."

The *Yehudi HaKadosh* said, "The Master's words are like glowing coals, and they can't be swallowed quickly."

The *Chozeh* was preoccupied with the coming of *Mashiach*. He, Rebbe Menachem Mendel of Rimanov, and the Maggid of Kozhnitz felt that they could intensify their prayers to bring *Mashiach*. When the Napoleonic wars broke out, these three *tzaddikim* wished this to be the "battle of Gog and Magog," which was to be followed by the coming of *Mashiach*. When Napoleon invaded Russia, they prayed for his victory. Rabbi Shneur Zalman of Liadi prayed that Russia triumph. He said that a victory by Napoleon would result in eliminating all the discriminatory laws against Jews, and this would result in widespread assimilation. "Better to suffer anti-Semitic decrees than to lose our people through assimilation."

> *Rabbi Shneur Zalman's words were prophetic. In the United States, where Jews have equal opportunities, intermarriage has reached unprecedented proportions, and the number of people who identify themselves as Jews has dwindled drastically.*

In the spring of 1815, Rebbe Menachem Mendel of Rimanov died, but the *Chozeh* felt that he and the Maggid of Kozhnitz could intensify their prayers adequately to force the coming of *Mashiach*.

On Succos, 1815, the Maggid of Kozhnitz died, but his disciples, knowing how dear he was to the *Chozeh*, kept this news from him, and it was not revealed to him by *ruach hakodesh*. On Simchas Torah, the *Chozeh* was jubilant during the *hakafos* (Torah processions), and retired to his room to rest a bit, asking his rebbetzin to watch him.

When the rebbetzin heard a child crying, she left the room momentarily; when she returned, the *Chozeh* was not there, She asked the chassidim to go out and look for him, but their search was fruitless. One chassid strayed far off, and upon hearing groaning, asked, "Who is here?"

A soft voice responded, "Yaakov Yitzchak ben Devorah Meitel."

The chassid then rushed back for help, and they carried the *Chozeh* home. He took to his bed, from which he did not arise, passing away on *Tishah B'Av*.

The *Chozeh* said, "I did not know that the Maggid of Kozhnitz had died, and on my own I was unable to defend myself against Satan. If the Maggid had not spread his cloak to catch me, I would have been crushed."

What happened to the *Chozeh* remains a mystery. There was only a small window in his room, through which egress was impossible. In addition, bottles on the windowsill had not been disturbed.

Rebbe Zvi Elimelech of Dinov (*Bnei Yisasschar*) said, "Every Rosh Chodesh *Nissan* [first day of the month of *Nissan*], the *Chozeh* would write what was going to transpire every month of the year. In the last year, he wrote only until the month of *Av*, the month in which he passed away."

The *Chozeh* was a Levite, and traced his ancestry back to Korach. He said that Korach was a great person who made a grave error in opposing Moses. The *Chozeh* referred to Korach as "my holy grandfather, Korach."

The *Chozeh* said, "I am a *Levi*, and the *Leviim* sang in the *Beis HaMikdash*. Alas! I cannot sing, but if I were able to sing, I would cause such a craving in Heaven for the song of the *Leviim* that Hashem would restore the *Beis HaMikdash*."

Teachings

The *Chozeh's* teachings are found primarily in three *sefarim*: *Divrei Emes, Zikaron Zos,* and *Zos Zikaron*. Many of his teachings can also be found quoted in the works of his disciples.

The Talmud cites the verse "*Shavas vayinafash* — He rested and was refreshed," and comments, "*Kevan sheshavas, vy avdah nefesh* — Once one has completed the Sabbath, 'Woe! He has lost the extra *neshamah* that one has on Shabbos'" (*Beitzah* 16a). The *Chozeh* asked, "Why do we say this verse on Friday night at the beginning of Shabbos? It is more appropriate at the close of Shabbos."

The *Chozeh* said that another interpretation is possible. "*Kevan sheshavas* — once Shabbos enters — *vy avdah nefesh* — the *nefesh loses the vy* [woe].'" As we say in the *Bircas HaMazon* on Shabbos, "Grant us respite from all our anguish." Shabbos eliminates the "woe."

When a person repents his sins and vows never again to disobey Hashem's will, Hashem forgives him and makes him like a new being, so that his previous sins no longer result in any evil desires.

When a person does sincere *teshuvah,* he comes very close to Hashem. He then feels greater shame for having sinned and becomes extremely humble. This humility enables him to bind himself to Hashem on a higher level, which in turn results in even greater shame for having gone against Hashem's will, This leads to further humility and a stronger attachment to Hashem, resulting in an infinite spiritual growth.

☞ One of Baal Shem Tov's disciples complained that he was very frustrated. "I try to bring myself close to Hashem, and just when I feel He is within reach, I suddenly find myself more distant than before."

The Baal Shem Tov said, "That is as it should be," and told him the following parable.

A father wishes to teach his infant son to walk. When the child is able to stand upright, the father places himself close to the child, extends his hands to within a few inches of the child, and beckons him to come. Although the child is fearful of falling, he feels it is safe to try because his father is close enough to catch him, so he ventures the first step. The father then retreats a little and again beckons to the child, who, seeing that he did not fall and that the father is still close, has the courage to take another step. The father retreats progressively further, and the child, seeing that he has not fallen, continues to advance.

If one could read the child's mind, one would see that the child is thinking, "What is going on here? The harder I try to reach my father, the farther away he gets."

The fact is that the father and the child have disparate goals. The child's goal is to reach the father. The father's goal is to teach the child how to walk. If the child were to reach the father, there would be no further progress.

"So it is with you," the Baal Shem Tov said. "You wish to reach Hashem, but Hashem's goal is for you to grow and advance spiritually. If He were to allow you to reach Him, your growth would come to an end."

Spiritual growth is infinite."

The *yetzer hara* (evil urge) may sometimes masquerade as a saint, teaching piety, repentance, and self-denial. We must be on the alert for the *yetzer hara's* cunning. For example, it may try to convince us that another person is a scoundrel, and that it is a mitzvah to take revenge on him.

> A man once told the *Tzaddik* of Sanz that someone had undercut him in business and caused him to lose a great deal of money. The man was very angry and said that he would retaliate. The *Tzaddik* told him that the Torah forbids taking revenge.
>
> The man said, "That does not apply in this case. This person is a *rasha* and it is a mitzvah to bury him."
>
> The *Tzaddik* said, "That is incorrect. The Midrash says the Jews in Egypt were bereft of mitzvos, so Hashem gave them the two mitzvos of *korban Pesach* [the paschal offering] and *milah* [circumcision]. By performing these two mitzvos they would merit the miracles of the Exodus.
>
> "However, Rashi says that the plague of three days of darkness came about because some Jews were *reshaim* and died because they did not wish to leave Egypt. Hashem inflicted three days of total darkness, so that the Egyptians would not see the Jews being buried [*Exodus* 10:22].
>
> "In that case, why does the Midrash state that the Jews were bereft of mitzvos? They buried the *reshaim*, didn't they? Obviously," the *Tzaddik* said, "burying a *rasha* is not a mitzvah."

At other times, the *yetzer hara* may tell one to do *teshuvah* by practicing self-denial. On careful scrutiny, one may discover that this is just to make a show of piety. Sometimes the *yetzer hara* may urge self-mortification to make one weak, thus preventing him from serving Hashem properly. A person may be misled by the *yetzer hara* and think that what he is doing is proper.

One must, therefore, pray intensely that Hashem should give him the proper sense to do what is right.

☞ The Chofetz Chaim used to go into the *beis midrash* late at night and order the *talmidim* (students) to go to sleep. He said that their drive to learn into the early hours of the morning does not come from the *yetzer tov*, but rather from the *yetzer hara* that wants them to be so exhausted the next day that they will not be able to concentrate.

The Chofetz Chaim pointed out that we pray, "Remove Satan from before us and from behind us." The "before us" is understandable, because Satan may stand in the way of one's doing mitzvos, but what does "behind us" mean? The Chofetz Chaim says that sometimes Satan stands behind a person and pushes him to do mitzvos; e.g., learn until 3 a.m. so that one is tired the next day, fast so that one will be weak, give away everything one owns to *tzeddakah* so that he becomes destitute. So we ask that Hashem protect us from Satan pushing us from behind.

The Psalmist says, "For with You there is forgiveness, so that You should be feared" (*Psalms* 30:4). In what way does forgiveness lead to fear of Hashem?

If there was no forgiveness, then a sinful person would not mend his ways. For what purpose? Without forgiveness one is doomed to carry the burden of one's sins forever, and there would be no motivation for *teshuvah*. However, since there is forgiveness, a person knows that even if he has sinned, he may still come close to Hashem, and he will fear doing anything that will preclude his bonding with Hashem.

When Moses prayed for forgiveness after the sin of the spies, (*Numbers* 14:20), Hashem said, "I have forgiven according to your words." Moses pleaded that if Hashem were to destroy the Jews for their lack of faith in Him, the Egyptians will say that He did so because He was unable to conquer the land of Canaan for them. In other words, Moses asked for forgiveness to avoid a *chilul Hashem* (desecration of His Name). If a person sincerely asks for forgiveness so that it increases the glory of Hashem, he will be forgiven.

> *Chassidic writings are replete with the concept that ideally prayer is not intended to ask for things for oneself, but for Hashem's sake, as King David says, "Not for our sake, Hashem, not for our sake, but for Your Name's sake give glory" (Psalms 115:1). In the davening we often say, "Do for Your sake if not for ours." Even when we ask for healing, it is because "You are the faithful and compassionate Healer," i.e., to give glory to Your Name as a healer.*
>
> *The sefarim point out that when one asks for something for himself, his record may be examined to see if he deserves to receive it. However, if one does not pray for himself, but for Hashem's sake, then there is no reason to question if that person is deserving.*
>
> *In the Amidah we pray, "We hope for Your salvation all day long." "Your salvation" should not be understood as "the salvation You provide for us," but rather Your salvation, because when Jews are in exile, the Shechinah is in exile, and we pray for the*

> *Shechinah.* The Psalmist says, "I [Hashem] am with him in distress" (Psalms 91:15), and the Talmud says that when Jews suffer, Hashem says, "My head is heavy and My arm is heavy." The ideal prayer, then, is to relieve the *Shechinah* of its suffering.

◦ A lumber merchant complained to his Rebbe that after he had invested in a forest, the price of lumber dropped, so that he suffered a financial loss. The Rebbe said, "The Talmud says that when Jews suffer, Hashem suffers with them. Now tell me, is it worthwhile to put the *Shechinah* into misery because of a few pieces of wood?"

It is very difficult to be able to set one's own needs aside and pray for Hashem's sake, but it is a spiritual goal which one should pursue.

We pray, "Bring us back to You, Hashem, and we shall return; renew our days as of old" (*Lamentations* 5:21). "As of old" refers to Creation, at which time there were no merits to bring about Creation. The Midrash says that Hashem foresaw the mitzvos that *tzaddikim* would do, and these merits brought about Creation. In other words, Hashem invoked the merits of the future.

We pray to Hashem for forgiveness, not because we deserve it, but because if we will be forgiven, we will be able to do mitzvos properly, and we thus invoke the merits of the future. So we say, "Bring us back to You, Hashem, and we shall return; renew our days as of old." Just as before Creation You considered the merits of the future, so, too, if You forgive us now and bring us back to You, we will do Your will in the future.

> *When Moses prayed to be permitted to enter Eretz Yisrael, the Torah uses the expression* וָאֶתְחַנַּן *(I implored); Rashi says that this refers to a prayer for Hashem's grace. Even though tzaddikim could pray using the merit of their good deeds, they ask only for grace (Deuteronomy 3:23). The commentators remark, "Why would a tzaddik invoke his own merits? Tzaddikim never feel that they have done enough." They answer, "A tzaddik does not invoke the merits of the good deeds he has done, but the good deeds that he will do when Hashem helps him."*

☞ A man complained to the *Chozeh* that he had *machshavos zaros* (alien thoughts) that interfered with his *davening*.

The *Chozeh* said, "Why do you call these '*machshavos zaros*'? They are not alien. They are very much your own.

"If a *tzaddik* has interfering thoughts during *davening*, they are indeed *machshavos zaros*. If an unpleasant odor is detected in the king's palace, then one must look for its source. However, if one's house is next to a tannery, of course there will be unpleasant odors.

"If you keep your mind free of objectionable thoughts at all times, they will not bother you during *davening*."

The *Chozeh* said, "*Tehillim* states, 'Hashem will count in the writing of nations' [*Psalms* 87:6]. What does that mean?

"The counting in *Lashon Kodesh* [Hebrew] is different than that of the nations. In *Lashon Kodesh* there are no digits. Numbers are words, e.g., *echad* [one], *shtiyim* [two], etc. In the writings of other nations, there is the digit 'zero,' which does not exist in *Lashon Kodesh*.

"'Zero' has no value. A whole string of zeros is still nothing. However, if you put a '1' in front of a string of zeros, it can be an astronomical number.

"If you *daven* without *kavannah*, it is a nothing, a zero, and you accumulate a string of such zeros. Then, one day, you *daven* or do a mitzvah with real *kavannah* — you have put a '1' in front of the zeros, and they add up to a significant amount.

"That is what is meant by 'Hashem will count in the writing of nations.' Hashem will use the zero of other nations so that your *tefillos* without *kavannah* can one day add up to a great amount."

Niflaos HaRebbe in *Sefarim Kedoshim*

The Chozeh cited the *berachah*, "Who has sanctified (betrothed) us with His commandments and took pleasure in us." The *sefarim* say that the relationship of Hashem to *Klal Yisrael* is like a marriage, in which Hashem is the husband and *Klal Yisrael* is the wife. That is the meaning of "He bethrothed us." For a marriage to take place, the *chasan* must give the *kallah* something of value. But we say that Hashem betrothed us with mitzvos, and mitzvos are something *we* give to Hashem. The Talmud says that if the *kallah* gives something of value to the *chasan* instead of receiving something from him, the marriage is not valid. How then can it be that the item of value for the marriage between Hashem and *Klal Yisrael* is the mitzvos, which we give to Him?

However, the Talmud makes an exception. If the *chasan* is a highly honored person who generally does not accept gifts, his accepting the item from the *kallah* is actually perceived as his giving her something.

Inasmuch as Hashem takes pleasure in our performance of the mitzvos, we are pleased that He is willing to accept our mitzvos, and this satisfies the requirement that the *chasan* must give something to the *kallah*.

This is the meaning of the *berachah*, "He betrothed us with His mitzvos." But how can our mitzvos be a vehicle for the *kiddushin*? Because Hashem takes pleasure in our mitzvos, and we are so grateful that He is accepting our mitzvos that His acceptance of them is a gift to us.

☞ Rebbe Elimelech once went to the Maggid of Mezeritch, and the *Chozeh,* who was then a young man, asked to accompany him. On Shabbos, the *Chozeh* sat at the far end of the table. The Maggid cited the story in the Talmud (*Avodah Zarah* 17a) of Elazar ben Durdia, who had been a profligate sinner all his life. When he had a moment of enlightenment, realizing that he had led so depraved a life, he began to do *teshuvah*, pleading for mercy, and wept uninterruptedly. He died while weeping. A voice from Heaven proclaimed, "Rebbe Elazar ben Durdia is invited to *Olam Haba*." The Talmud states that Rebbe Yehudah HaNasi wept, saying, "It is possible for a person to acquire *Olam Haba* in so brief a period."

"Why did Rebbe cry?" the Maggid asked. "This seems like something one would be happy about. Perhaps Rebbe wept because had Elazar ben Durdia lived after he did such profound *teshuvah*, he could have done mitzvos at a very high level."

At the far end of the table, the *Chozeh* whispered to his neighbor, "I have a different explanation." The neighbor conveyed this until it came to the ears of the Maggid, who said, "Let me hear what the young man has to say."

The *Chozeh* said, "The Talmud says that on the day that Rebbe Yehudah HaNasi laughed, something bad would occur. Maharsha explains that Rebbe Yehudah HaNasi had taken upon himself to suffer for *Klal Yisrael* in order for them to merit forgiveness. If anything detracted from his suffering, that protection of *Klal Yisrael* was suspended, and something bad would happen. When Rebbe Yehudah HaNasi heard that it is possible for a person to acquire *Olam Haba* in a brief period, he was actually overjoyed, but he realized that if he allowed himself to feel happy, he would be distracted from his suffering, and something bad would happen. Therefore, he wept in order to subdue his joy."

The Maggid said, "The young man's explanation is better than mine."

> *The person who conveyed this story to me said that the Maggid's interpretation is actually that of the Maharsha in Avodah Zarah 10, and that his statement that the Chozeh's explanation was better than his was due to his humility.*

☞ A miserly man never gave any *tzeddakah*. One day, his son fell seriously ill, and his brother-in-law prevailed upon him to send a *kvitel* and a donation to the *Chozeh*. The man grudgingly did so. When the brother-in-law gave the *kvitel* to the *Chozeh*, the latter gave the child a *berachah* and said, "The Talmud says that if a person gives *tzeddakah* 'in order that my child may live,' he is a complete *tzaddik* [*Pesachim* 8a]. This can also be read as 'he *will be* a complete *tzaddik.*' From now on, this man will give *tzeddakah.*" Indeed, the man became a *baal tzeddakah*.

Stories

I heard the following story from a cousin in Israel who was 103 years old. She was a descendant of Rebbe Nachum of Mekarov, who married the *Chozeh's* granddaughter, Hinda.

At the wedding, the master of ceremonies announced the gifts that were being given to the newlyweds. The *Chozeh*, deep in meditation, did not respond. Someone asked him, "Does the Rebbe wish to give the couple a gift?"

The *Chozeh* replied, "Yes, I give myself!"

Several years later, after the *petirah* (death) of the *Chozeh*, the couple had a boy, whom they named Yaakov Yitzchak. People who remembered the *Chozeh* said that the child bore a striking resemblance to him. The child's right eye was larger than his left eye, just as the *Chozeh's* was. There was no doubt in anyone's mind that the child had the *neshamah* of the *Chozeh*.

The *Chozeh* took two disciples and traveled to the town of his childhood. On Friday night, they waited in shul for someone to invite them for Shabbos, as was the usual practice. However, no one invited them, until the last person remaining in shul, an elderly man, said, "You may come to my home. I don't have much to offer you, but you can share what I have." They joined the man, and although the food was sparse, they celebrated the Sabbath with *zemiros* and Torah discourses. The man spread out some straw to serve as a mattress for them.

The next day, after they had eaten, the man asked them where they came from, and they said, "Lublin."

The man's eyes brightened. "Lublin?' he said. "Do you know a Reb Yaakov Yitzchak in Lublin?'

The *Chozeh* said, "Yes, we know of him."

"I hear that he is a great *tzaddik*," the man said. "I was his *melamed* in *cheder*. He was not a bad child, but he used to run away from *cheder*, and I beat him for that. Then, one day, I was walking through the woods and I saw Yaakov Yitzchak sitting on the grass, his arms extended toward the sky, and repeating, 'G-d is One. G-d is One.' I knew then that he was a holy child, and I never beat him again.

"Now he is a famous *tzaddik*. I cannot travel to Lublin. How I wish I could see him before I die and ask for his forgiveness."

The *Chozeh* then said, "I am Yaakov Yitzchak, and I forgave you a long time ago. You were only trying to discipline me."

The *melamed* and his student embraced tearfully. After Shabbos was over, they took their leave of their host.

Sunday morning, en route to Lublin, the *Chozeh* said, "We must return to my *melamed*."

When they arrived at the *melamed's* home, they found that he had died during the night. The *Chozeh* saw to it that his *melamed* was given a respectful funeral.

Another version of this story states that the childhood *melamed* was Rebbe Avraham Abli, an authoritative kabbalist. He greatly admired his prodigious student, Yaakov Yitzchak, and felt a loss when the family moved away.

In his late years, Rebbe Avraham Abli would pray tearfully at the end of a meal, "*Ribono shel Olam!* I once had a holy student. Please, let me know what happened to him." His prayers were accepted, and the *Chozeh* was Divinely inspired to visit his *melamed*.

The *Chozeh* invited himself to the *melamed's* home for Shabbos. After the meal, Rebbe Avraham Abli said his usual prayer to see his holy student. The *Chozeh* said, "Rebbe, do not agonize over this. I can show you who this child is — it is I."

"But who are you now?" Rebbe Avraham Abli asked.

"I am the Rebbe of Lublin."

Rebbe Avraham Abli was overjoyed, and said, "Now that I have the *zechus* to have the great Rebbe of Lublin in my home, I will gather some of my friends to greet you."

The *Chozeh* said, "*Chas veChalilah!* (G-d forbid!) You must promise not to reveal my identity to anyone."

On Shabbos, the townsfolk saw that Rebbe Avraham Abli was exuberant, but no one knew why. After *havdalah*, the *Chozeh* bade his *melamed* farewell and left.

After the *Chozeh* left, Rebbe Avraham Abli felt that he was now free to tell people who his guest was. When they heard that it was the *Chozeh,* they hurried after him and caught up with him.

They asked, "Why did you conceal yourself from us?"

The *Chozeh* said, "And who revealed my identity to you?"

They said, "Rebbe Avraham Abli."

The *Chozeh* cried, "Woe! I tried to extend his life, but he forfeited it!"

They returned to give Rebbe Avraham Abli his deserved last respects, and the *Chozeh* eulogized his teacher. "If only he had not exposed my identity, he could still have lived."

When the *Chozeh's* father discovered that the young Yaakov Yitzchak was spending time in the woods, he asked him why he was going into the woods. "To find Hashem," the child said.
"But Hashem is the same everywhere," the father said.
"But I am not," the child answered.

A group of chassidim hired Tzadok, a wagon driver, to take them to Lublin. Tzadok was devoid of learning, but, as a member of the community, observed Yiddishkeit. En route, the people wrote their *kvitlach* to submit to the *Chozeh*. Tzadok asked them what they were doing, and they explained that one gives the Rebbe a petition listing one's needs. "Write a *kvitel* for me, too," Tzadok said. The chassidim asked his name and his mother's name and wrote a *kvitel*.

Tzadok dropped his passengers at the Rebbe's home and went to buy a beer. When the chassidim gave Tzadok's *kvitel* to the *Chozeh*, he said, "Who is this person who shines so brightly in Heaven?"

The chassidim were stupefied. *Tzadok shines brightly in Heaven?* Could it be that Tzadok was one of the hidden *tzaddikim*, who was masquerading as an ignoramus? They dispersed throughout Lublin to find Tzadok. Eventually they came to an inn where there was a wedding party, and there was Tzadok, dancing on the table, making merry for the guests.

The chassidim took Tzadok aside. "Tell us the truth about yourself," "they demanded. "You are one of the hidden *tzaddikim*!"

Tzadok roared with laughter. "Me? A hidden *tzaddik*? Why, I can hardly even read the *siddur*!"

"What are you doing at this wedding party?" they asked.

Tzadok said, "I stopped here for a beer, and I saw that they were prepared for a wedding, but everyone was glum. The *chasan* said that he had been promised a *tallis* with a silver *atarah* [ornamentation], but the *kallah's* father had not made good on his promise, and the *chasan* would not go to the *chuppah* without the *tallis*. The *kallah's* father said that he had no money for a *tallis* with a silver *atarah*. The wedding was in danger of being canceled, so I took out all my money and sent someone to buy the *tallis*. They went on with the wedding, and invited me to join them — and that's why I'm here."

Tzadok's mitzvah — enabling the wedding to proceed and preventing the pain and humiliation that might have resulted — was a *zechus* that caused him to shine in Heaven.

Chassidim of yore had great trust in the Rebbe, following the Rebbe's instructions even when they did not understand them.

One of the *Chozeh's* chassidim complained that he was unable to find a *shidduch* for his daughter because he could not afford a dowry. The *Chozeh* told him to travel to a certain town, and Hashem would enable him to acquire adequate money for a dowry. The chassid had no idea what he was to do in that town, but his *emunas tzaddikim* (trust in the counsel of a *tzaddik*) was firm. He traveled to that town, rented a room in an inn, and spent the entire day in Torah study.

After several weeks, seeing that this tenant did not engage in business, spent the day in Torah study, and *davened* with great *kavannah*, the innkeeper became curious and started a conversation with him, eventually asking him why he had come to that town.

The man said, "Truthfully, I don't know what I am to do here, but the Rebbe of Lublin told me that if I came here, Hashem would provide me with a dowry for my daughter, so here I am."

The two men became friends, and the innkeeper told the tenant that he earned his *parnassah* from the inn. "I was once a merchant and did much business, but I suffered a setback recently," he said. "Following several profitable transactions, I had returned from Danzig with a large amount of cash. I sorted the cash into bundles of 1000, put my seal on the wrappings, and put them into my lockbox. I left for a short while, and when I returned, the lockbox was opened and the cash was gone. The only one who could have taken it was my servant, but he refused to admit it, even after severe beatings. Without capital I could do no more business, so now I make my livelihood solely from this inn."

Years before, the innkeeper had hired a *melamed* for his children, and even after the children grew up, he retained the *melamed*, providing him with free room and board. The *melamed* became friendly with the tenant, and told him how thankful he was to the innkeeper for his continued support. The tenant told the *melamed* that the Rebbe of Lublin had told him that Hashem would provide a dowry for his daughter if he came to this town.

One day, the *melamed* asked the tenant to take a stroll with him. "I think I know how you can get the money for your daughter's dowry," he said.

"I am deeply ashamed," the *melamed* continued, "but I must confess my sin. I had been here for several years, teaching the innkeeper's children, and he was always very kind to me, but I have been very cruel to him.

"Not long ago, I saw the innkeeper put money into his lockbox. I don't know what happened to me, but I was overcome by an uncontrollable impulse, and I took the money. Moments later, I realized what a terrible thing I had done and I was going to put the money back, but the theft had already been discovered and the whole household was in turmoil. The servant was suspected and was beaten brutally. I could not bring myself to admit that I had taken the money, because I was considered honest and trustworthy and I was above suspicion. I've been trying to think of ways in which I could return the money without revealing my crime. Just to leave it in the open would be unsafe, since so many people pass through the inn.

"Here is how you can help me. No one could possibly suspect you, because you were not here at the time. Here is the money. You can find a way to return it without implicating me."

The tenant returned to his room, and when the innkeeper came to talk with him, the tenant asked him to repeat the story of how his money had been stolen.

The tenant then said, "I can get the money back for you, but you must promise that you will not press me to tell you how I got it. You know that I certainly did not take the money, because I was not here at the time of the theft."

After the innkeeper promised, the tenant gave him the money he had received from the *melamed*. The innkeeper recognized the bundles, which still bore his seal. Tearfully, he embraced the tenant, and as a reward gave him the money he needed for the dowry.

"I don't understand how all this happened, but I believe that the Rebbe of Lublin engineered this so that I would get my money back and you would get the dowry for your daughter."

From *Emes Vyatziv, pp. 50-53)*

A chassid complained to the *Chozeh* that he had fallen on hard times. The *Chozeh* told him to go to the market in Berditchev. Although he had no idea what he was to do there, he went to Berditchev.

For several days, he walked through the marketplace. No one approached him with an offer to sell nor inquired what he had to sell. On Friday afternoon, a merchant approached and asked him what he wanted to buy.

"I'm not looking to buy anything. However, I wish to take you to a *din Torah*."

The merchant was from London. "A *din Torah*?" he asked. "Did I ever meet you before? Did you ever transact any business with me?"

"No," the man answered. "Nevertheless, I want to have a *din Torah* with you."

"Very well," the merchant said. "This makes no sense to me, but I cannot refuse a request for a *din Torah*. Obviously, we cannot have a *din Torah* today, but I will go with you after Shabbos."

On Sunday they came to Rebbe Levi Yitzchak of Berditchev. The man from Lublin said, "My father was a well-to-do merchant, but he left me no money. I told the Rebbe of Lublin that I was penniless, and he told me to go to the market in Berditchev. All week, not one person spoke to me. On Friday, this man asked me if I wanted to buy something. Inasmuch as he was the only person to talk to me, I believe that the Rebbe knew that somehow this person would be the source of my salvation. That's all I know."

"What kind of business did your father have?" Rebbe Levi Yitzchak asked.

"He sold honey wholesale, in great quantities. He died five years ago while away from home."

Rebbe Levi Yitzchak asked the London merchant, "Was your father a merchant?"

The man answered affirmatively, and added, "He, too, died away from home several years ago."

"Did he import foodstuff, such as honey?"

Again, the man answered affirmatively.

"Did you take an accurate inventory and an accounting after your father's death?" Rebbe Levi Yitzchak asked

"Yes," the London merchant said. "There was an excess of 3000 rubles, for which we could not account, and the money is held in escrow until we can determine to whom it belongs."

Rebbe Levi Yitzchak said to the London merchant, "Your father bought 3000 rubles worth of merchandise from this man's father, but he died before he had a chance to pay for it. The 3000 rubles belong to the man from Lublin, and the Rebbe from Lublin saw this."

> *Exodus 21:1 states, "And these are the ordinances that you shall place before them," introducing the laws of the Torah governing fiscal matters and damages. The Zohar comments, "This is the order of gilgul [reincarnation]." What does gilgul have to do with the ordinances in this parashah?*
>
> *The Psalmist says, "The judgments of Hashem are true, altogether righteous" (Psalms 19:10). An isolated judgment may not appear to us as righteous, but taken altogether, they are righteous.*
>
> *The sefarim say that there are cases in which a person dies owing money to another person. To correct this injustice, Hashem manipulates things so that the descendants of the debtor will somehow return the money to the descendants of the creditor.*

There is a story handed down in our family about our ancestor, the Rebbe of Cherkassy, who once lodged at the home of a chassid in another town. The Rebbe asked his host if he would do him a great favor.

The host said, "Rebbe, anything you ask for is yours."

"Good," the Rebbe said. "Let's go out to your stable." At the stable the Rebbe looked at several of the horses and said to the host, "I'd like you to give me that horse."

The host said, "Please, Rebbe, ask for any other horse, but not that one. That is my most reliable horse. It has pulled my wagon out of the deep mud more than a few times. I really cannot part with it."

"Very well," the Rebbe said, and they returned to the house. Eventually, the Rebbe directed the conversation to a person named Elia Nosson. He asked the host, "Did you happen to know Elia Nosson?"

The host said, "As a matter of fact, I did. Many years ago we were partners in a business."

"And what happened to the partnership?"

"We broke up," the host said. "We were just not getting along."

"Was the dissolution of the partnership handled fairly?" the Rebbe asked.

The host said, "Yes and no. Elia Nosson was supposed to buy me out, but he died before paying everything he owed me."

"Have you forgiven the debt?" the Rebbe asked.

The host said, "Not really. There was no one to forgive."

"Will you forgive it now?" the Rebbe asked. The host said, "Of course. What purpose is there in not forgiving it? He can never pay me back now."

"Good," the Rebbe said. "It is important that it be forgiven."

The following morning, the host found that his most reliable horse had died. The Rebbe told him, "The Heavenly Tribunal ruled that Elia Nosson must pay you what he owed you. He was reincarnated in that horse, which is why that horse served you so well. Once you forgave that debt, the horse had no reason to serve you."

This is why the Zohar comments that the verse, "And these are the ordinances that you shall place before them," is related to gilgul. It is through gilgul that some injustices may be corrected.

The *Chozeh* was upset because he did not have the opportunity to properly fulfill the mitzvah of *hachnasas orchim*, since no one came to his home to request food or lodging.

Late one winter night, a man from a nearby village came to Lublin to ask the *Chozeh* to pray for his wife, who was having a very difficult labor. The city was dark; it seemed that everyone was asleep. The man saw a light burning in one house and knocked at the door. The person who answered invited him in, and, since the man was shivering with cold, sat him near the fire and gave him a hot drink.

"What brings you here so late at night?" the host asked. The man said he had come to ask the *Chozeh* to pray for his wife, but that he did not know where the *Chozeh* lived.

"You can't go out in the cold this late at night," the host said. "Warm up a bit and sleep for a few hours, and in the morning you can go to the *Chozeh*. By the way, what is your wife's name? And her mother's name?" The man told him the names.

The host prepared a bed for the man. When he awoke, he said, "I must hurry to the *Chozeh*."

"No need to hurry," the host said. "I took care of that for you. The *Chozeh* said that your wife will be fine. Have some breakfast, and then you can go."

After the man ate, the host said, "*Mazal tov!* Your wife gave birth to a boy."

Upon leaving, the man found out that his host was the *Chozeh*. The *Chozeh* was grateful that Hashem had given him the opportunity to fulfill the mitzvah of *hachnasas orchim*.

> *The Chofetz Chaim once hosted one of the roshei yeshivah in his humble home and was preparing the bed for him. The guest was upset that the Chofetz Chaim himself was providing for his needs and said, "Please don't do that. I can do it myself."*
>
> *The Chofetz Chaim responded, "Tomorrow morning, when I put on tefillin, will you also say, 'Please don't do that?' Hachnasas orchim is a mitzvah like any other. Why should you want to stop me from doing a mitzvah?"*

In the town of Satria lived the great gaon, R' Aryeh Leib HaKohen, author of the classic work, *Ketzos HaChoshen*. Some of the *Chozeh's* chassidim lived in Satria, and R' Aryeh Leib, who was a misnaged, criticized their conduct, which he felt violated halachah.

The chassidim did not act respectfully to R' Aryeh Leib, who declared a 30 day *cherem*, resulting in the townsfolk shunning them. The chassidim chose to go to Lublin until the *cherem* expired.

The *Chozeh* told his *shamash* that these chassidim were barred from his court for two weeks, corresponding to the duration of the *cherem*.

When they were admitted after the *cherem* expired, the *Chozeh* said, "On the verse 'Why did you not fear to speak against My servant, Moses' [*Numbers* 12:8, when Aaron and Miriam were critical of Moses], Rashi comments, 'My servant, even if he was not Moses, and Moses, even if he was not My servant.' I understand that Hashem demanded that they revere His servant, even if he was not Moses. But why were they to revere Moses if he was not Hashem's servant?

"There are two kinds of *tzaddikim*," the *Chozeh* said. "One kind of *tzaddik* devotes every act, every movement, every moment of the day to the service of Hashem. There is another kind of *tzaddik* who excels in Torah study. There can thus be a servant who is not a Moses, and a great scholar, a Moses, who is not a servant.

"Your Rav, R' Aryeh Leib, is the outstanding Torah scholar of this generation. How dare you not relate to him with the utmost reverence?"

> *Kavod HaTorah, honoring Torah scholars, is required even when one does not agree with them*
>
> *Two chassidim of the Tzaddik of Sanz were in Pressburg on Passover, guests at the Chasam Sofer's table. Among chassidim, it is the custom to avoid eating gebroks (matzah that has come into con-*

tact with liquid). This is a chumrah (stringency) that misnagdim have not adopted; hence, the Chasam Sofer ate kneidlach on Passover.

When the chassidim were served kneidlach, they were in a quandary, because they had never eaten gebroks. One chassid did not eat the kneidlach. The other reasoned, "I'm sitting at the table of the gadol hador [the greatest Torah scholar of the generation]. Who am I to be more strict than he is?" and he ate the kneidlach.

When they reported their visit to the Tzaddik of Sanz, the latter said to the chassid who ate the kneidlach, "You have earned Olam Haba." To the chassid who had refused to eat them, the Tzaddik said, "You had better stand near me on Yom Kippur, and I will try to elicit forgiveness for you."

The latter's behavior was a violation of kavod HaTorah.

Rebbe Dov Ber of Ropschitz, a disciple of the *Chozeh*, lived in abject poverty. Before Pesach, on the night of *bedikas chametz*, his wife had to borrow a slice of bread from a neighbor so that she could put out the 10 pieces for the *chametz* search, but they did not reveal the extent of their poverty to anyone.

Erev Pesach, while Rebbe Dov Ber was still in shul, two men came to his home and told his wife that they were merchants en route, but would not make it home before Yom Tov. They said they were very meticulous about Pesach food, and could not stay just anywhere. Rebbe Dov Ber's wife said that she would be happy for them to stay in her home, but there was no food even for the family. The men went into town and returned with matzos, wine, and an abundance of food.

The men went to shul, and after *davening* they told Rebbe Dov Ber that they wished to spend the first two days of Pesach with him, knowing that he observed their standard of kashrus. Rebbe Dov Ber said that he had no food to offer them, and they said, "If you won't eat, then we won't eat."

When they arrived home, Rebbe Dov Ber saw that the table was set royally, and that these two men had provided everything. Rebbe Dov Ber was elated. They celebrated the seder with long discourses on the Haggadah, and the following two days were spent in Torah discussions. After *havdalah*, the two men abruptly departed.

On Shavuos, Rebbe Dov Ber was with the *Chozeh*, who asked him how he was faring. Rebbe Dov Ber told the *Chozeh* how fortunate he was to have had guests for Pesach who enabled him to have a true *simchas Yom Tov*.

The *Chozeh* said, "Fine guests, indeed. Those were the angels Michael and Gavriel! Henceforth, your mazal will shine and you will have ample *parnassah*."

> *Jewish Lublin no longer exists physically, but Jewish Lublin is preserved eternally in the Daf Yomi study established by Rav Meir Shapiro of Lublin, and in the heritage of the Chozeh, through the transmission of his Torah and the accounts of his life.*

Rebbe Avraham Yehoshua Heschel of Apta (1748-1825)

I cannot claim to be unbiased. I am privileged to bear the name of this illustrious ancestor.

When I visited the grave of my paternal grandmother, and read the inscription, "Fourth generation to Rebbe Avraham Yehoshua Heschel of Apta," I felt chills running up and down my spine. My grandmother was the great-granddaughter of this venerable *tzaddik*! I was overwhelmed with both great pride and apprehension.

Why apprehension? In the *Tochachah*, the severe reprimand wherein Hashem warns Israel of what will befall them if they deviate from the Torah, we read, "And I shall remember My covenant with Jacob, and also My covenant with Isaac, and also My covenant with Abraham" (*Leviticus* 26:42). Why are these words of great comfort included in the *Tochachah*, which speaks of the grave consequences of deviating from Torah?

Shelah explains that if two thieves are brought to court, one of whom was raised in a criminal environment and the other in a decent environment, the latter will be dealt with more harshly. The thief raised by criminals never learned that it was wrong to steal, whereas the thief raised by decent people was taught right from wrong. Because he ignored what he was taught, his sin is so much the greater.

Therefore, *Shelah* says, when Hashem judges us for our sinfulness, He will say, "Look where you came from. Your ancestors, Abraham, Isaac, and Jacob, were saintly people, and you should have followed in their footsteps. You are, therefore, more culpable than those who do not have a heritage of such outstanding saintly people." Our genealogy intensifies the gravity of our sinfulness.

That is why I was apprehensive. On my judgment day, the Heavenly Tribunal will say, "You were but the sixth-generation descendant of so holy a *tzaddik*, and yet your self-indulgent behavior was so far removed from the saintliness of your ancestor. You deserve a more severe punishment."

I am consoled only by the fact that perhaps this ancestor, whose *ahavas Yisrael* is legendary, will exercise this trait to intervene in my behalf and plead for mercy and leniency.

The Rebbe of Apta served as Rav of several communities, including Kolbasov, Apta, Iassi, and Medzhibozh. He promised the people of Apta that his name would always be associated with their community; hence he is known as the Rebbe of Apta.

The importance of *ahavas Yisrael* is hardly an innovation of Chassidic teaching. Hillel said that the essence of Torah is the mitzvah, "You shall love your fellow as yourself" (*Leviticus* 19:18). R' Akiva said that this is an all-encompassing principle of the Torah. Nevertheless, the emphasis that Chassidus puts on *ahavas Yisrael* is unparalleled.

> *Someone asked the Baal Shem Tov, "How can it be a mitzvah to love Hashem? We cannot see or touch Him, and we cannot understand anything about Him. How can one develop love for an abstract concept?"*

> *The Baal Shem Tov said, "Develop great love for your fellow Jew. That will lead you to love of Hashem."*

The Rebbe of Apta left instructions that no words of praise be inscribed on his tombstone. The only inscription permitted was, "*Oheiv Yisrael*," (one who loves his fellow Jews) — the title of his work on the *parshiyos* of Torah.

The Rebbe of Apta had an illustrious lineage. He was named after an ancestor, the renowned Rebbe Heschel, the teacher of R' Shabsi HaKohen, one of the greatest halachic authorities, generally referred to as the *Shach*, the title of his commentary on the Shulchan Aruch.

☞ The Rebbe of Apta related, "When I was Rav in Kolbasov, I noticed two strangers who had come to town. I invited them for tea and cake, and returned to my Torah study. The two were conversing, and although I tried to concentrate on what I was studying, I could not help overhearing them, and it seemed that they were discussing some very important topics.

"They asked if I could put them up for the night, and although I lived in cramped quarters, I made room for them. They left the following morning.

"I began to reflect on what I had overheard, and realized that they were discussing things of the highest order of *kedushah*. I regretted that I had not been more respectful to them.

"Two weeks later, I saw a coach passing by, and these two men were in it. I ran after them and tried to enter into conversation with them, but they said that they were hurrying and had no time to talk with me. I asked what I could do for them, and they said that I could get them a bagel. I gladly did so, but they had already gone. I ran after the coach and reached them. I said that I wanted to learn from them, but they replied, 'You do not belong to us. Your place is in Lizhensk with Rebbe Elimelech.'

"I later learned their identity: Rebbe Levi Yitzchak of Berditchev and Rebbe Moshe Leib of Sassov."

The Rebbe of Apta studied at the yeshivah of the outstanding *gaon,* Rebbe Shmelke of Nikolsburg. The Rebbe of Apta told the following story about the Master.

☞ Rebbe Shmelke never slept in a bed. He studied Torah day and night, and when he felt drowsy, he would rest his head on the *shtender* for a few minutes of sleep.

Once, upon awakening from his few minutes of sleep, Rebbe Shmelke was in the dark because his candle had extinguished. He went to the window to see if there was any light in a neighboring house from which he might be able to relight his candle. At the window, someone handed him a burning twig, he lit the candle, and returned to his studying.

After a few moments, he thought, H*ow could anyone have reached the window?* He was on second floor of the house! He prayed for revelation to know who handed him the fire, and it was revealed to him that because his Torah study was so dear to Hashem, Hashem had sent the prophet Elijah to light his candle. Rebbe Shmelke began crying, regretting that because of him, Elijah had been "disturbed," and he fasted to atone and obtain forgiveness for this "sin." The Rebbe of Apta would say, "Look at what these *tzaddikim* considered to be 'sins.'"

☞ One Purim, the Rebbe of Apta received money from his admirers, and his son, Rebbe Yitzchak Meir, saw the Rebbe polishing the coins.

"Father," he said, "you always despise money. Why are you polishing the coins now?"

The Rebbe answered, "Today there is a mitzvah of giving money to the poor. If money has no value to me, then I would be giving them something worthless. So, I'm polishing the coins to make me feel they have some value."

☞ The Rebbe of Apta came to a town and found that they were observing a fast day because of a drought. He said, "You need rain so that the crops will grow, but when you fast you show Hashem that you can get along without food. Better to serve a meal and discuss Torah, to show Hashem that you are dependent on food, and must have food to be able to study Torah."

As was noted, Rebbe Elimelech bequeathed his power of speech to the Rebbe of Apta. This was manifest not only in the fiery style of his discourses on Torah, but also in his strange exaggerations in his descriptive speech. Just as in the Talmud we find stories that are impossible, and contain hidden meanings (for example, see the stories of Rabbah bar Chanah in *Bava Basra* 73-74), so also the exaggerations of the Rebbe of Apta contained hidden meanings.

Rebbe Dov of Ropschitz said, "I served one hundred twenty *tzaddikim* who had *ruach hakodesh*, but none of them carefully weighed every single word in a golden scale the way the Rebbe of Apta did."

This concept was also expressed by the great *gaon*, Rebbe Yitzchak Meir of Gur (author of *Chiddushei HaRim*): "I never encountered any speech that was as pure as that of the Rebbe of Apta."

☞ The *tzaddik*, Rebbe Meir of Apta (author of *Ohr LaShamayim*), visited the Rebbe of Apta, who told him how his *beis midrash* was built, grossly exaggerating when describing an absurd quantity of building materials that he said had been used.

Rebbe Meir said, "I was able to understand the hidden meanings in all his exaggerations until he spoke about the windows, but then he lost me."

☞ Rebbe Yitzchak of Radville, the son of Rebbe Michele of Zlotchow, became a *mechuten* (related through the marriage of their children) with the Rebbe of Apta. Before the wedding, Rebbe Yitzchak had a dream, in which his father told him, "Listen carefully to the Rebbe of Apta's exaggerations. They are all kabbalistic secrets."

Upon listening to each of the Rebbe of Apta's exaggerations, Rebbe Yitzchak said, "This story was an explanation of a very difficult passage of the *Zohar.*"

The Rebbe of Apta said, "It is not much of a trick to know that if you have a father who tells you everything."

☞ Two men had been close friends from childhood on. After each was married, they entered into business as partners, and the business was very successful. The wife of one of the men disliked the wife of the other partner, and incited her husband against his partner, saying that the latter's wife was making him take an unfair share of the profits. It came to the point that one partner said to his friend, "We can no longer remain partners," and they divided the business.

The second partner grew more successful, and the other partner's wife was jealous and malicious. She hired two witnesses to testify that the former partner's wife had committed adultery.

When the witnesses testified before the Rebbe of Apta, he thought a bit, then summoned his son, Rebbe Yitzchak Meir, and told him, "Go and announce that the Rav of Apta is a fraud! No one is to consult him, and no one is to give him any money.

"The Torah says that we must accept the testimony of two witnesses, and what the Torah says is absolute truth. These two witnesses testified against this woman, but I can see that she is innocent. If what I see conflicts with what the Torah says, I am a fraud." The Rebbe wept, "I am a fraud! I am a sinner!"

The two witnesses were so shocked that they confessed that they had been bribed to give the false testimony.

The Rebbe of Apta often spoke about *Mashiach*. "We will be more deserving of the Redemption than previous generations. In the days of the Temple, *beis din* had the ability to punish sinful people, so their observance of Torah was really not a matter of free choice — the penal code acted as a deterrent. But today, there are no deterrents and no shame. A person can be openly sinful yet be a respected citizen. Anyone who observes the Torah does so by free choice, and that is why our generation is more deserving."

> *This idea is a great zechus for our generation, which has declined far more than that of the Apta Rebbe's generation. Today there are not*

only no deterrents to sin, but corruption and iniquity are applauded. By this standard, it is possible that we are truly a more deserving generation!

- The Rebbe of Apta said, "*Ribono shel Olam*! I know I am sinful and deserve to be in *Gehinnom*. But I really don't want to be in the company of people who committed grave sins. So, please let everyone out of *Gehinnom* so that You can put me in."

At the end of *Deuteronomy*, the verse reads, "So Moses, servant of Hashem, died there, in the land of Moab" (34:5), and in the beginning of *Joshua* the verse says, "And it was after the death of Moses, servant of Hashem (1:1)." Why is Moses referred to as "the servant of Hashem" in relation to his death?

The Rebbe of Apta explained, "The Midrash relates that Moses submitted 515 prayers to Hashem to allow him to enter Eretz Yisrael. Hashem said to Moses, 'This is the land which I swore to Abraham, to Isaac, and to Jacob, saying, "I will give it your offspring"' (*Deuteronomy* 34:2). Rashi comments, 'Go tell the Patriarchs that I fulfilled My promise to them.' Moses was thus given a mission by Hashem, and he accepted his death in order to enable him to tell the Patriarchs that Hashem had fulfilled His promise to them. Thus, even in his death, Moses served Hashem as His messenger."

- One morning, when the *shamash* knocked on the Rebbe's door as he summoned people to *davening*, the Rebbe awoke with an extraordinary passion to serve Hashem.

    He asked the *shamash*, "What was in your mind when you knocked on my door?"

The *shamash* said, "I don't know any esoteric *kavannos*. We are simple people, and what my father taught me was that as I knock on the door three times, I should say, 'Abraham, Isaac, and Jacob.' So that's what I do."

The Rebbe said, "The *shamash's* sincerity in invoking the names of the Patriarchs awakened my desire to serve Hashem."

☞ The *Chozeh* of Lublin had a disciple, Reb Aharon Moshe, who was unable to tolerate the presence of a sinful person. By looking at a person, he was able to know everything about that person, and the word spread that he had this unusual power.

He came to the Rebbe of Apta, who said, "I understand that you share the vision of the *Chozeh*."

"What can I do?" Reb Aharon Moshe replied. "I can see through a person."

The Rebbe of Apta said, "In my younger years, I, too, had that ability. I could tell how many reincarnations a person had been through and knew everything he had done from the day he was born. But I decided that it is not good to be able to see all the wrongs a person has done, and I prayed to Hashem to take away that power. Now, when a person comes before me, I see him as he is now, and I focus on all the good he has done.

"My advice to you, Reb Aharon Moshe, is to pray to Hashem to divest you of this power, so that you should not see what should not be seen."

☞ When the rabbinical position in the town of Kolbasov became vacant, the townsfolk began the search for a Rav. In the chronicles of Kolbasov it was specified that every candidate for the position must spend a Shabbos with the *parnes* (head of the community). If he satisfied the tests put to him by the *parnes*, he was qualified for the position of Rav of the town.

It so happened that the *parnes* at that time was a wealthy man who had obtained the position because he was the prime support of the community. This man was ignorant of Torah, but considered himself to be a scholar. When he tested the candidates, he asked them ridiculous questions that they were unable to answer, so they were disqualified.

When Rebbe Avraham Yehoshua Heschel applied for the position, he was hosted by the *parnes*, who said to him, "I can see that the Rav is a scholar, so I will ask you this question. Where is the source that Laban wished to sacrifice Abel [Hevel]?"

It was all the Rav could do to refrain from laughter. He quickly understood what this ignoramus was referring to, and he acted as if he were in deep thought. He realized that the Haggadah says that Laban "wished to uproot all — בִּקֵּשׁ לַעֲקוֹר אֶת הַכֹּל." There must have been a misprint in the *parnes'* Haggadah, so that instead of the word הַכֹּל (*hakol*), it read הֶבֶל (*hevel*). Thus, the *parnes* had concluded that Laban had desired to kill Abel (Hevel). He therefore gave the Haggadah as the answer to the *parnes'* question.

The *parnes* was thrilled. Finally, here was a candidate who was a true Torah scholar! The Rav was then elected the Rav of Kolbasov.

Years later, when the Rebbe of Apta would relate this episode, he said he was grateful to Hashem for enabling him to grasp what was in the *parnes'* mind. He cited the Midrash commenting on the verse in *I Kings* (5:11), "King Solomon was wiser than all persons," explaining that he was wiser even than fools. It takes great wisdom to understand a fool.

R' Avraham Yehoshua Heschel, *HaRav M'Apta*, Chaim Yehudah Berl

> *Actually, the Midrash states that Solomon was wiser even than the* shotim, *which is accurately translated as "deranged" rather than "fools." From my work as a psychiatrist, I can testify that it is a major challenge to understand what goes on in the mind of a deranged individual. Sometimes one may not discover for years what that person meant, and then his or her distorted logic becomes clear.*

☞ The Rebbe of Apta held the Rebbe of Rizhin in very high esteem. The Rebbe of Rizhin attended a wedding in Ostilla. He was a young man of 17, whereas the Rebbe of Apta was 60. During the dancing, the Rebbe of Rizhin's *gartel* (sash) fell to the ground. The Rebbe of Apta bent down, picked up the *gartel*, and wrapped it around the 17-year-old Rebbe of Rizhin, saying, "Hashem has given me the opportunity to do *gelillah* [wrapping] on a *sefer Torah*."

Teachings

Following the principle established by Rebbe Elimelech of Lizhensk, the Rebbe of Apta speaks of the centrality of the *tzaddik* and the importance of cleaving to a *tzaddik*.

When Hashem gave us the Torah, He gave it to us with all His powers, so that with the Torah, the *tzaddik* can achieve all the powers of Hashem. Therefore, with the strength of the Torah, a *tzaddik* can bring forth the sustenance and provisions for all mankind, and can bring all sorts of remedies, peace, grace, and kindness to the world.

The confessions and prayers of the *tzaddikim,* who confess on behalf of *Klal Yisrael*, open the paths whereby the prayers [of *Klal Yisrael*] can reach into heaven.

By virtue of the fact that people support the *tzaddik*, they, too, can be elevated, and together with the *tzaddikim* of the generation, they can cleave unto Hashem.

The *tzaddik* has no desire other than to bring blessings and beneficence to *Klal Yisrael*, so that they should have no lacks and no suffering …. The *tzaddik* has no personal desire, having cast off all earthly desires, which mean nothing to him … and because of his love for Hashem is ready to sacrifice his life for Hashem.

"A *tzaddik* may experience a spiritual decline, but this is in the interest of spiritual elevation. When a *tzaddik* experiences a descent, it enables him to better understand the needs of people and to attract the proper blessings for them.

The Rebbe of Apta warns against associating with "evil people" because the corrupt thinking of the latter may impact upon him. It may be that the Rebbe was referring to the *haskalah* (enlightenment movement), which sought to undermine observance of the Torah.

In *Proverbs* 2:5 it states, "If you will explore for it as for silver, and search for it as for treasure, then you shall understand what fear of Hashem is." The Rebbe of Apta says that one should learn fear of Hashem by emulating the wealthy, who are never satisfied with the wealth they have, but constantly strive to increase it. Similarly, that is how *tzaddikim* act, never satisfied with the mitzvos and good deeds they have done, but always striving to do more.

"Just as a person may have fine oils and wines, but if he has no containers for them they will all go to waste, so too, if a person has wisdom, understanding, knowledge, and even fine traits, if he lacks *yiras Shamayim*, all will be for nought, because *yiras Shamayim* is the container that will preserve all of these."

On Purim, my father would relate the following excerpt from *Oheiv Yisrael*.

> We read in the *Megillah* that when Esther pleaded for her people, saying, "I and my people have been sold 'to be annihilated, killed, and destroyed,'" Ahasueros asked, "Who is it that dared to do this?" Why did he ask? Didn't he remember that Haman had asked for a royal decree to annihilate the Jews and that he had approved this? Furthermore, Esther then added, "Had we been sold into slavery, I would have been silent" (*Esther* 7:4). Why was that necessary? What was the purpose of volunteering that she would have accepted enslavement?
>
> The Rebbe of Apta relates a story. There was a very wealthy man who owned a *sefer Torah* that had been written by the prophet Ezra the Scribe. When the man died, each of his two sons wanted the Torah.

One son said, "Instead of dividing the estate equally, you can take 60 percent of the estate, and I will take 40 percent and the Torah."

The other son said, "No, let's do it just the other way. You take 60 percent and I'll take 40 percent plus the Torah"

The first son then offered, "You may take 75 percent," and his brother said, "No, you take 75 percent."

Eventually, each one was willing to forgo his entire inheritance in order to gain possession of the Torah. It was finally resolved by *beis din*, which awarded the Torah to one son and the entire fortune to the other.

In that town, there was a priest who was a *meshumed* (convert to Christianity). He could not make peace with this incident. He had abandoned Judaism, yet here in his town was a person to whom Ezra's Torah was so dear that he gave up a great fortune for it. The priest's guilt ate away at him. His anger was so great that he decided to damage the Torah, rendering it unfit for use. He concealed himself in the shul, and after everyone left, he took out the *sefer Torah*, and in the verse that reads "You shall serve your G-d" וַעֲבַדְתֶּם אֶת ה' אֱלֹקֵיכֶם , he erased the letter ע and wrote an א in its place. By doing so, the meaning *"serve"* וַעֲבַדְתֶּם is replaced with *"destroy"* וְאִבַּדְתֶּם thus inserting a false blasphemic phrase in the Torah.

When this portion of the Torah was read, the people were horrified to discover this terrible error. How could Ezra the Scribe have made so gross an error? Even if the mistake were to be corrected, the Torah would not be exclusively

Ezra's writing. The Torah was designated as *pasul* (defective) and was set aside.

The son who owned the Torah was devastated. He took it so to heart that he fell sick. His father appeared to him in a dream and said, "G-d forbid that Ezra would have made such an error. This is the work of the *meshumed*, who erased the ע and wrote in an א. Because he took out an *ayin*, ע(*ayin* = eye), he will lose his eyesight. Insofar as correcting the *sefer Torah*, Ezra himself will come down from *Gan Eden* to correct it, and the entire Torah will be in his handwriting."

The following day, they checked the Torah, and indeed, it had been corrected, and the *meshumed* had become blind.

"What happened in *Megillas Esther*," the Rebbe of Apta said, "was exactly this. Haman obtained a decree from Ahasueros to enslave the Jews, and the decree said *l'avdam* with an ע. Haman then erased the ע and wrote in an א, which changed the meaning to 'to destroy them.' This is why Esther said to Ahasuerosh, "I do not challenge your decrees. If the decree had been as you had approved, to enslave the Jews, I would have accepted it. But your decree was altered to read 'to destroy the Jews' rather than 'to enslave them.' That is why Ahasueros said, "Who dared do this? I had never agreed to a decree to destroy them." Esther then said, "It was the wicked Haman who falsified your decree."

Another Torah comment of the Rebbe of Apta that my father quoted was on the verse, "Let the earth sprout vegetation: herbage yielding seed, fruit trees yielding fruit after its kind" (*Genesis* 1:11). Rashi comments that Hashem's command was that the earth should produce a fruit tree such that the tree itself (i.e., the trunk and branches) would have the taste of its fruit, but the earth did not do this. Rather, although the earth produced a fruit-bearing tree, the tree itself did not taste of its fruit. Therefore, when Adam was punished for his sin, the earth was also punished for its disobedience.

One may ask, "How could the earth sin?" It is usually explained that this refers to the angel whom Hashem designated to care for the earth.

The Rebbe of Apta asks, "Why would the earth disobey Hashem? It has no *yetzer hara* that incites it to sin. Furthermore, if the earth deserved to be punished, why was the punishment delayed until Adam sinned?"

The Rebbe explained, "The earth [i.e., its ministering angel] foresaw that man was destined to sin, and feared that Hashem would destroy the world. Therefore, it committed a sin by disobeying the command of Hashem. Inasmuch as man would be formed out of earth, there could be a defense that because he was made of a substance that had sinned, he was prone to sin. This would mitigate man's punishment. Therefore, the punishment for the earth was delayed until Adam was punished for his sin, because the earth itself was implicated in Adam's sin."

My father would also quote the following.

The Torah says that Noah entered the ark "because of the waters of the flood" (*Genesis* 7:7). Rashi comments that Noah was weak in his belief; i.e., he believed but did not believe that there would be a flood, until the waters of the flood forced him to enter the ark.

The Rebbe of Apta asks, "How can one say that Noah, whom the Torah describes as 'a perfect *tzaddik*,' was weak in his belief?"

The Rebbe of Apta explains that the word *maamin*, which means "belief," also can mean "to raise," as is written in *Megillas Esther* (2:7) that Mordechai brought up (*omein*) Esther. Thus, *emunah* is so powerful that with firm *emunah* one can bring on that which one believes. Therefore, although Noah certainly believed Hashem when He said that there would be a flood, he intentionally vacillated in his belief, lest a firm belief would actually hasten the flood.

One of the *tzaddikim* said that when Rashi came up to heaven, all the *tzaddikim* came forth to greet him, except for Noah, because Rashi had written that Noah was weak in his belief. When the Rebbe of Apta explained that Noah intentionally vacillated in order to avoid hastening the flood, Noah came to greet Rashi.

Someone asked the Rebbe of Apta, "The Torah says that Jacob worked for Laban for seven years to marry Rachel, and that the seven years were like just a few days because of his love for her. That is not logical. For a person who is separated from someone he loves, each day is a century. How can the Torah say that 'the seven years were like just a few days'?"

The Rebbe of Apta said, "Most often when a man loves a woman, it is really himself that he loves, and his feeling for the woman is because she gratifies his needs. In that case, separation is a deprivation of his needs, and each day is a century. Jacob did not love himself. He loved Rachel, not as an object that would gratify him. It was a selfless love, an appreciation of the other person. In a selfless love, seven years can be like a few days."

The Rebbe of Apta said, "A widow came to my Master and was complaining of her misery. The Master spoke to her in comforting words, but began to weep. I, too, began to weep, when I realized that the Master was really referring to Jerusalem, of which it is said, "The city that was great with people has become like a widow" (*Lamentations* 1:1).

The Talmud cites the verse, "This is the Table that is before Hashem" (*Ezekiel* 41:22), and comments, "Inasmuch as Ezekiel is talking about the Altar, why does he refer to it as 'the Table'? This tells us that as long as the *Beis HaMikdash* existed, the offerings on the Altar effected atonement. In absence of the *Beis HaMikdash*, a person's table effects atonement" (*Berachos* 55a).

The Rebbe of Apta explains, "When a person eats not for gustatory pleasure, but to obtain the nourishment that enables him to study Torah and perform mitzvos, he thereby elevates the Divine spark that is within the food; this is equivalent to an offering on the Altar."

The Rebbe of Apta emphasizes the importance of *emes* (truth).

"A person should develop love for *emes*, so that in all one's actions and in all one's deeds, one does not deviate from *emes* and *yashar* (uprightness, integrity). If a person realizes that everything in the world derives from the truth of Hashem's existence, and that the existence of the world is based on *emes*, and furthermore, that every living person has a soul that was breathed into him by the Source of *emes*, one would see it is proper that one's desire and goal should be to attach oneself to the Source of *emes*."

> *All of the sifrei mussar and Chassidus stress the importance of truth and point out that the primary tactic of the yetzer hara is to make falsehood appear to be truth.*
>
> *Delusions are false ideas, and the yetzer hara deludes people. Doesn't a person understand that material wealth cannot bring happiness? Yes. Then why do people sacrifice their health and lives to attain wealth? Because the yetzer hara deludes them — and delusions are sronger than reality.*
>
> *Why do intelligent people sometimes make self-destructive choices? Because the yetzer hara deludes them, so that they do not see the reality of their choice. The drug addict knows that drugs are detrimental, and in a lucid moment knows that he should not use them, but the yetzer hara tells him that drugs will make him happy.*
>
> *Inasmuch as we are always inclined to do what we believe will be pleasurable and are always under the influence of the yetzer hara, how can we ever know what truth is?*
>
> *The answer is that inasmuch as Hashem is absolute truth, if we identify with Hashem, we will be identifying with truth. How does one identify with Hashem? By emulating Hashem's middos (Rashi, Deuteronomy 13:5; Sotah 14a), to be kind, forgiving, slow to anger, and humble. These are the very middos that the yetzer hara discourages, rendering us vulnerable to being deluded.*

It is known that the Patriarch Abraham was the embodiment of *chesed* (kindness) and that Isaac was the embodiment of *gevurah* (stern justice). This enables us to understand the dialogue of Abraham and Isaac as they went to the *Akeidah* (*Genesis* 22:7). "Isaac spoke to his father and said, "Father —" "and he [Abraham] said, "Here I am, my son."

The Rebbe of Apta interpreted the dialogue thusly. Isaac said to his father, "Father"; i.e., you are the embodiment of *chesed*. How will you be able to bring me as an offering?" Abraham responded, "Here I am, my son"; i.e., I am now like you, my son, functioning with *gevurah* (stern justice).

The Torah says, וְהָיָה עֵקֶב תִּשְׁמְעוּן אֵת הַמִּשְׁפָּטִים הָאֵלֶּה — *This shall be the reward when you hearken to these ordinances* (*Deuteronomy* 7:1). The Rebbe of Apta said, "The word וְהָיָה implies 'in the end,' and the Torah is saying, 'Ultimately, you *will* hearken to these ordinances,' so, why delay? Why not do so now?"

The prophet says, חֲכָמִים הֵמָּה לְהָרַע וּלְהֵיטִיב לֹא יָדָעוּ — *They are wise to do harm, but not to do good*" (*Jeremiah* 4:22).

Regarding an oath, the Torah says "Or if a person will swear ... to do harm or to do good" (*Leviticus* 5:4). The Talmud comments that "to do good" means to take an oath that "I will eat," and "to do harm" means to take an oath that "I will not eat."

The Rebbe of Apta explicates Rashi's comment: "They are wise to do harm" — they only know how to serve Hashem by fasting and self-mortification; they are not wise enough "to do good" — to serve Hashem by eating and partaking of the good in the world.

The Talmud says that the verse upon which all service of Hashem depends is "Know Him [Hashem] in all your ways" (*Proverbs* 3:6). We should serve Hashem not only by performing mitzvos, but in everything we do. A person may eat to satisfy his palate, or he may eat with the intention that the nourishment will enable him to do mitzvos. In the latter case, eating is in the service of Hashem.

According to the Rebbe of Apta, the prophet criticizes those who do not dedicate all their actions to the service of Hashem, mistakenly thinking that it is achieved only by self-deprivation.

"Do good, Hashem, to good people, and to the upright in their hearts" (*Psalms* 125:4)

The Psalmist says, "Hashem is close to all who call upon Him — to all who will call upon Him in truth" (*Psalms* 145:18). This verse appears to be paradoxical. It begins by saying that Hashem is close to *all* who call upon Him, without qualification, then goes on to qualify the statement, adding, 'to all who will call upon Him in truth.'

The first statement means that Hashem responds to the prayers of all persons when they pray, but not necessarily when they have a wish for something and have not yet prayed for it. However, when *tzaddikim* are involved, Hashem responds to their wishes even *before* they have been verbalized in prayer, as we say in *Aneinu*, "And it will be before they call, I will answer."

This is what the Psalmist says, "Do good, Hashem, to good people, and to the upright in their hearts" — to the upright, the *tzaddikim*, even when their wishes are in their hearts, before they have been verbalized in prayer.

The Rebbe of Apta discouraged fasting as a means of atonement. He said, "If I had the authority, I would eliminate all fast days except Tishah B'Av and Yom Kippur. Tishah B'Av — how can anyone eat on that bitter day? Yom Kippur — who needs to eat on this glorious, sacred day?"

The Torah says וַיֵּרָא אֵלָיו ה' בְּאֵלֹנֵי מַמְרֵא — literally, "Appeared to him [Abraham] Hashem in the plains of Mamre …" (*Genesis* 18:1). The Ohr HaChaim remarks that it would have been appropriate to put the subject before the predicate: וַיֵּרָא ה' אֵלָיו — literally, "Appeared Hashem to him."

The Rebbe of Apta quoted Rebbe Moshe of Pshevorsk, who explained the verse as follows: *Tzaddikim* always feel that they have not done enough to warrant closeness to Hashem, and that others have achieved greater spirituality than they have. So it was with Abraham, who felt that his friend, Mamre, had advanced to a closer relationship with Hashem, but that he himself was just at the onset, still distant.

The verse then reads, וַיֵּרָא אֵלָיו ה' בְּאֵלֹנֵי מַמְרֵא וְהוּא יֹשֵׁב פֶּתַח־הָאֹהֶל — It appeared to Abraham that בְּאֵלֹנֵי מַמְרֵא ה' the — *Shechinah* was with Mamre, who had already achieved a closeness to Hashem, whereas he himself was וְהוּא יֹשֵׁב פֶּתַח־הָאֹהֶל — only at the door to the tent of *kedushah*, not yet having entered it.

With this interpretation, the Ohr HaChaim's question is answered. The verse reads, "It appeared to him," with the subject before the predicate.

The Rebbe of Apta pointed out the gravity of *lashon hara*. Of all the seven "shepherds" — Abraham, Isaac, Jacob, Moses, Aaron, Joseph, David — the only one who has the title "*Tzaddik*" is Joseph, who is regularly referred to as *"Yosef HaTzaddik"* because he was able to withstand the attempted seduction by Potiphar's wife. Yet, it was his *lashon hara* about his brothers that led to our ancestors' enslavement in Egypt. On the other hand, Judah, who did not deny

Tamar's claim, but instead publicly admitted the truth, to his own embarrassment (*Genesis* 38:26), was rewarded with the kingship of Israel and with a descendant who will be *Mashiach*.

A man complained of his troubles to the Rebbe of Apta. The Rebbe said, "Hashem will help you."

The man said, "But Rebbe, what do I do until Hashem helps?"

The Rebbe smiled. "Hashem said to Jacob, 'I will not forsake you until I will have done what I have spoken about you' [*Genesis* 28:15]. So with you: Hashem will not forsake you before He helps you."

Stories

A man said to the *Tzaddik* of Apta, "Rabbi, I have difficulty with the passage that Hashem can lower the highest person down to earth. Take me, for example. I am very wealthy. I own profitable factories and valuable real estate. Even if something were to happen to my personal wealth, my children are independently wealthy. Furthermore, I am a highly respected citizen of the community. Hashem would have to cause widespread disaster to bring me down. I do not deny that Hashem is all-powerful, but it is not reasonable to suggest He would turn the world upside down in order to humble me."

The *Tzaddik* said, "You speak unwisely. One does not question Hashem."

Time after time, the man told the *Tzaddik* that this thought did not allow him to have peace of mind. How would Hashem humble him? Finally, the *Tzaddik* said, "Hashem can do anything."

Later that day, the man was overtaken by an obsessive thought that he must convert to Christianity. He tried to banish this absurd thought from his mind, but it only became more intense and tormented him. Finally, he could not restrain himself, made his way toward the church, and told the priest that he wanted to convert.

The priest said, "Are you mocking me? I know who you are. You are a leading citizen in the Jewish community. You cannot be serious. This is some kind of a trick."

The man began to plead with the priest, and tearfully insisted that he was sincere in his desire to convert.

"I have difficulty believing that you are sincere," the priest said. "You must prove it to me by signing over everything you own to the church."

The man could not help himself. The priest drew up a document stating that he was converting to Christianity and was turning over everything he owned to the church. The man signed the document, and the priest locked it in his desk drawer.

"Wait here," the priest said. "I will return soon and I will perform the conversion."

As soon as the priest left, the man fell into a deep sleep, and awoke after a few minutes. Discovering himself in a church, he said, "What am I doing here?" and promptly jumped out the window. He remembered all that had transpired. "What did I do?" he said. "I am penniless. Everything I owned now belongs to the church. And my children will not even look at me — their father — a *meshumd* [apostate]! There is nothing more odious in all Judaism than a *meshumd*, someone who renounced Judaism. And the community? Why, they will despise me! I will be shunned more than a leper!"

Bewildered and in utter despair, he walked the streets. It then occurred to him to go to the *Tzaddik*. The *Tzaddik* greeted him warmly and said, "But Hashem can do the second half of the verse, too: 'and [He] lifts the lowly.' Just listen."

They heard a tumult outdoors, and when they went out to see the cause, they saw that the church was aflame. It burned to the ground, along with the desk and the document. There was no indication of the man's misadventure.

It is my practice to recite the *Kaddish* following *Kaballas Shabbos*. This is based on a family tradition, as related by my father.

The *Tzaddik* of Apta lived in poverty, like most of the rabbanim in the villages. One Erev Succos, he had no money to buy even the most meager provisions for the festival. He told his wife that under no circumstances was she to ask anyone for money, neither as charity nor as a loan. He then went to the *beis midrash* to study Torah.

After the *Tzaddik* left, a man came to his home, and told the rebbetzin that he was a merchant on the way home from a business trip, but that he could not reach home before sundown. "I'm carrying a large sum of money with me, and I want to stay somewhere where I can be assured of safety. I assume that the rabbi's home would be the safest place, and I would like to stay here for Yom Tov."

The rebbetzin said, "I would gladly have you as our guest, but we have nothing to offer you. We do not even have challah or wine for the meal."

"That's not a problem," the man said. "Here is some money. Go to the market and buy everything needed for Yom Tov." The man then left to purchase an esrog and lulav.

When the *Tzaddik* returned from shul and saw that the succah was lit up, he could not understand how this could be, since they had no candles. His first thought was the rebbetzin could not resign herself to a barren Yom Tov and had accepted help from someone.

When the *Tzaddik* entered his house, the rebbetzin introduced the merchant who had given her money to buy provisions. The *Tzaddik* was delighted that Hashem had provided him with provisions for Yom Tov, and when the merchant showed him that he had bought an esrog and lulav, the *Tzaddik* was beside himself with joy, and he embraced the man.

As they sat down to the meal, the *Tzaddik* said to the man, "Would you mind moving down a bit?" When the man moved down, the *Tzaddik* said, "A bit farther down, please," and continued this until the merchant was at the other end of the table.

After the meal, the merchant said to the *Tzaddik*, "Rebbe, you owe me nothing. I bought everything because I needed a place to be on Yom Tov. Now, if other people were in the succah, I could understand that they are more deserving than me and should sit closer to you. But since there was no one in the succah except for the two of us, why did it bother you if I would have sat next to you?"

The Rebbe embraced the merchant and said, "My dear child, you have no idea how precious you are to me. But what do you mean that there was no one else in the succah? What about the Ushpizin [the spiritual Succos guests]? There must be a place for them."

When the man heard that he was in the presence of the Ushpizin, he was ecstatic. The following morning, he promptly sat at the far end of the table.

The next day, the merchant said, "Rebbe, if I have been privileged to be in the succah with the Ushpizin, I want to see them."

The *Tzaddik* said, "No, my dear friend, you cannot see them. One cannot continue to live after he has seen the Ushpizin."

The next day the merchant said, "Rebbe, I am over 60. I don't know how much longer I will live. I agree to die earlier. It is worth it to see the Ushpizin."

The *Tzaddik* tried to dissuade him, but the man persisted. Finally, on Hoshana Rabbah, the *Tzaddik* allowed him to see the Ushpizin.

The very next day, the man became ill. He said to the *Tzaddik*, "I know I am going to die, but I do not regret it. It was worth it. I have only one concern. I am childless, and there is no one who will say *Kaddish* for me."

The *Tzaddik* said, "I will say the *Kaddish* for you."

"And the *yahrzeit*?" the man asked.

The *Tzaddik* said, "I will observe the *yahrzeit*."

"And after the Rebbe's lifetime, who will observe the yahrzeit?"

The *Tzaddik* thought a bit, then said, "I will leave instructions to my descendants that the *Kaddish* Friday night after Psalms 92-93 should be recited in your memory."

And so, as a descendant of the *Tzaddik* of Apta, I say this *Kaddish* on Friday night, in memory of the guest who enabled the *Tzaddik* of Apt to celebrate a joyous Succos.

The Rebbe of Apta cited the Talmud that sharply condemns judges who accept bribes.

"I was once a member of a *beis din* for a *din Torah* of several days' duration. One day I felt a change of heart, and I realized that I was favoring one of the litigants. Since I could not be neutral, I withdrew from the *beis din*, but I had no idea of the reason for my bias.

"Several days later, it was *Rosh Chodesh* [first day of the new month] and I put on a different kaftan. I found something in the pocket. Unbeknownst to me, one of the litigants had put money into my kaftan pocket, as a bribe. Even though I was unaware of it, the bribe had affected my neutrality, and I favored that litigant.

"If this can happen when the judge is unaware of the bribe, how much more so is one biased when one knowingly accepts a bribe! How true are the words of the Talmud that harshly condemns someone who accepts a bribe."

A great deal has been written about the chassidim–misnagdim controversy. As a preface to the following story about the Rebbe of Apta, I wish to relate a story my father often told, which gives us a perspective on that episode in Jewish history.

The Baal Shem Tov once came to Brod, and when the great Torah scholars of the Kloiz (study group) of Brod, all of whom were zealously anti-Chassidus, became aware of his coming, they decided to harass him. The *gaon* Rav Chaim Tzanzer was by nature a pacifist, and he remained in the Kloiz and did not join his colleagues in persecuting the Baal Shem Tov.

That day, a woman came to Rav Chaim with a *she'ilah* (halachic query) regarding *taharas hamishpachah* (marital relations) and he ruled that the *she'ilah* was kosher.

Before retiring at night, Rav Chaim would review everything that had transpired that day. When he rethought the *she'ilah*, he concluded that his ruling was wrong. Realizing that a wrong ruling resulted in someone committing a transgression, Rav Chaim was heartbroken.

Rav Chaim then began to reflect on what could have caused him to give a wrong ruling. What sin had led to this? He concluded that his dereliction in not joining his colleagues in persecuting the Baal Shem Tov was the sin that led to his erring in halachah. To rectify this dereliction, he decided that he had to pursue and harass the Baal Shem Tov. He filled his pocket with stones with which to pelt the Baal Shem Tov.

Rav Chaim looked in at various inns, trying to find the Baal Shem Tov. By the time he reached the inn at which the Baal Shem Tov was lodging, it was dawn, and the Baal Shem Tov was reciting the morning *berachos*. When Rav Chaim saw the Baal Shem Tov, he could not bring himself to throw stones.

When the Baal Shem Tov finished saying the *berachos*, he greeted Rav Chaim. "Broder Rav," he said, "you agonized for nothing. Your ruling was in fact correct." He then proceeded to prove why the ruling was correct.

Rav Chaim felt relieved, and as he left, he emptied his pockets of the stones he had collected to pelt the Baal Shem Tov.

(When my father came to this part of the story, he would choke up with tears.)

The Baal Shem Tov picked up each stone, kissed it, and put it in his pocket. "Stones that were collected with *kedushah*," he said, "dare not roll in the dust."

That is what the early misnagdim were like. The chassidic and misnagdic giants were all saintly people.

Wherever the Rebbe of Apta traveled, he was always accompanied by his personal *shochet*. He would not eat meat provided by any other *shochet*. Whichever community he visited, he sent his *shochet* to the local Rav to show him the *chalef* (the knife used in *shechitah*, ritual slaughter), to obtain his approval.

When the Rebbe of Apta came to Leipnick, where the Rav was the *gaon* Rav Baruch Frenkel (author of *Baruch Taam*), he sent the *shochet* to the Rav. When the *Baruch Taam* checked the *chalef*, he found it had several defects. He asked the *shochet* to re-examine the *chalef*, and the *shochet* said that it was perfect.

The *Baruch Taam* had the *shochet* wait in another room. He placed the *chalef* on a sheet of paper and marked the spots where he had felt roughness. He then called in the local *shochet* and asked him to examine the *chalef*. The *shochet* said, "This is not a *chalef*. It is a saw!" The Rav asked the *shochet* to point out the rough spots, and they were exactly where he had found them.

The *Baruch Taam* called in the Apta Rebbe's *shochet* and said, "You must promptly desist from *shechitah*. It is clear that you have lost the sense of touch essential to prepare a proper *chalef*." He showed him that both he and his *shochet* had found the *chalef* grossly defective.

The *shochet* went back to the Rebbe of Apta and broke into tears. "I was not aware that I had lost my sensitivity of touch. I have been *shechting* with a defective *chalef*, and I have caused countless people to eat *tereifah*!' He wept so bitterly that he fainted.

The Rebbe of Apta revived him and said, "Heaven forbid! There is nothing wrong with your *chalef*. It was Hashem's will that the *Baruch Taam* should be a misnaged. So, to make him disparage me, Hashem sent down the Angel Michael to stand on the edge of the *chalef* to make it feel rough, so that the *Baruch Taam* should think that chassidim are lax in the observance of kashrus."

How little we understand about the chassidim–misnagdim controversy!

It is of interest that the *Baruch Taam*'s son-in-law was none other than Rebbe Chaim Halberstam, the *Tzaddik* of Sanz. The *Baruch Taam's* son, Yehoshua Heschel, became a chassid of the *Chozeh*. In his later years, the *Baruch Taam*'s attitude toward Chassidus underwent a change.

A man once came to the Rebbe of Apta, saying that he had committed a sin and asking what he should do for *teshuvah*. Instead of responding, the Rebbe simply jeered at him. The man began crying, but the Rebbe continued to jeer. Finally, the man retreated, sat down, and tearfully started saying *Tehillim* (*Psalms*).

Observers were taken aback by this behavior. They knew of the Rebbe's unparalleled *ahavas Yisrael*, yet here he mocked a person who was asking for guidance in doing *teshuvah*. Noticing their puzzlement, the Rebbe explained.

"You know that in a previous *gilgul*, I was a *Kohen Gadol*. Similarly, in a previous *gilgul*, this man had committed a sin for which he had to bring a sin-offering. When he bought the sheep, the farmer asked him, 'Why do you need this sheep? What kind of sin did you do?' and the man felt humiliated.

As he walked his sheep to the *Beis HaMikdash*, some children ran after him, shouting, "'You're bringing a sin-offering, huh? What did you do?' and he felt terrible.

When he entered the *Beis HaMikdash*, the Levites were playing a melody that just tore at his heartstrings. When he brought the sheep to me to bring as an offering, I looked at his tear-stained face, and I pitied him. He had almost achieved the full contrition that would have earned him full forgiveness.

"Because I felt so sorry for him, I tried to comfort him. I wept along with him, telling him that Hashem understands that a person may be overcome by a powerful temptation, and other such comments to restore his composure. That was a serious mistake. His sin weighed less on him, I interfered with his full contrition, and he did not achieve full forgiveness.

"His *neshamah* came down again to this world, and this is the same man now asking how to do *teshuvah*. I did not repeat my mistake. I jeered at him, and he felt intense remorse. Just look at him. He is saying *Tehillim* tearfully, praying with all his heart for forgiveness, which he will achieve. I am kinder to him now than I was then."

When the Rebbe of Apta was Rav in Kolbasov, there was a man who leased an inn from a *poritz* and fell behind on his rent. The *poritz* threatened that unless he paid the arrears immediately, he would send his agents to teach him a lesson. When he was unable to come up with the money, the *poritz's* henchmen came to the man's house, broke his windows, and tore apart his mattresses, letting him know that this was just a taste of what they would do unless he paid the money he owed.

On Shabbos afternoon, the man went to hear the Rebbe's *derashah* (sermon). He heard the Rebbe say that there are two *berachos* of redemption; one is *ga'al Yisrael,* in the past tense, which refers to the redemption from Egypt, and the other is *go'eil Yisrael*, in the present tense, which means that even when a *poritz* threatens to ruin someone, a person should have trust that Hashem will help him.

The man ran home in a state of ecstasy and began dancing, repeating, "The Rebbe said, '*Go'eil Yisrael*'! The Rebbe said, '*Go'eil Yisrael*'!"

When the *poritz's* henchmen came and saw the man singing and dancing amidst the ruins of his house, they reported to the *poritz* that the man had gone insane.

The *poritz* sent for the man and said, "Why are you such a ne'er-do-well? Go to my distillery, and give them this slip. They will give you a supply of liquor on credit. Sell it, and you will make enough money to pay the rent."

The man followed through and made a handsome profit. He then came to the Rebbe of Apta with a donation. "This is '*Go'eil Yisrael*' money," he said.

A chassid of the Rebbe of Apta told him that he had a daughter of marriageable age, and that he could not begin to provide a dowry for her. Without a dowry, he would not be able to find an appropriate *shidduch*.

"How much money do you need?" asked the Rebbe of Apt.

"Three hundred rubles," was the reply.

The Rebbe wrote a letter to a wealthy acquaintance, saying, "The bearer of this letter is a worthy person who comes from a fine family, who has suffered a serious financial reversal, and, because he lacks the money for a dowry, is unable to find a fitting *shidduch* for his daughter. Please give him 300 rubles on my account, and for this mitzvah you will be blessed with great prosperity."

When the wealthy man read the Rebbe's letter, he said, "What does he mean, 'on my account'? I never did any business with him, and I never borrowed any money from him. How can he ask me to give you 300 rubles? That is absurd. I can give you 10 rubles, and you can raise the rest by going to other people who are wealthier than I."

When the chassid turned down the offer, the wealthy man agreed to give him 20 rubles, then 30, but not 300. The chassid took back the letter and reported his failure to the Rebbe of Apta.

The Rebbe said, "I will give you a letter to someone else in another town," and wrote an identical letter to this second person.

When the chassid presented the Rebbe's letter to the second person, he said, "I don't have 300 rubles at the moment, but stay with me for a few days while I try to put together that sum." After several days, he gave the chassid 300 rubles. The chassid returned home, and was able to find a fine *shidduch*.

From that day on, the second man's business prospered, and he became very wealthy, while the first man's business deteriorated to the point that he became penniless and had to go begging. Walking on foot and hitchhiking rides, he came to the Rebbe of Apta.

When he entered the Rebbe's home, he broke into tears and exclaimed, "I want a *din Torah* with the Rebbe. Why has he punished me? True, I did not do his bidding, but in what way was I obligated to give a stranger such a huge sum of money?"

When the Rebbe heard the tumult, he came out to see the cause.

"Who are you?" he asked.

"Doesn't the Rebbe recognize me? I am the person to whom the Rebbe sent a letter several years ago, telling me to give someone 300 rubles."

The Rebbe said, "Of course, if I am summoned to a *din Torah*, I will go. But first, you should rest a bit. You are weary from such an exhausting trip." The Rebbe had him served a fine meal and provided him with a place to sleep.

The following morning, the Rebbe assembled a *beis din* and the man presented his case. "The Rebbe sent me a message to give this man a large sum of money 'on his account.' The Rebbe has no account with me, so why was I obligated to give this stranger 300 rubles? I was willing to give him 50 rubles, but he refused to take it. I did not feel that the Rebbe had any right to make such a demand of me 'on his account,' which does not exist, and then punish me so severely for not complying with his request."

The Rebbe then presented his case. "The Talmud says that 40 days before formation of the fetus, the fate of that fetus is announced, whether it will be strong or weak, bright or dull, poor or rich [*Niddah* 16b]. When it was decreed that I will be wealthy, I protested, because preoccupation with money would distract me from serving Hashem properly, but the angel said that a decree cannot be revoked.

"I said, 'If so, I want to put my wealth in safekeeping with several other people, with the understanding that if I should need to, I can withdraw some of it. This man's wealth was that which I had allotted to him. When he refused my request, I took the share that I had given him and gave it to another person. He should have understood that when I said 'on my account' I was not talking foolishly.'"

The *beis din* awarded the Rebbe the judgment, but asked him to forgive the man. The Rebbe did so, and blessed him with prosperity. Indeed, the man became wealthy once again.

The Rebbe of Apta's first position was in Kolbasov. He moved to Iassi and subsequently to Medzhibozh. He then resided in Apta for a number of years, after which he abruptly announced that he was returning to Medzhibozh.

The people of Apta were stunned. They and asked, "Why is the Rebbe leaving us? We have been devoted to the Rebbe, and we gave you double the wages that you received in Medzhibozh, as you requested. Have we in any way offended the Rebbe?"

The Rebbe said, "Heaven forbid! You have never offended me in any way! I will tell you why I am leaving.

"My father was a poor *melamed* in a town quite far from Apta. He had a brother, but the two were separated for many years.

"My uncle, who lived here in Apta, was well to do, but had no children. When he fell sick, he said to his wife, 'Inasmuch as we have no children, when I die, you will be unable to remarry because you will require *chalitzah*.' [The Torah provides that if a man dies childless, his brother should either marry the widow or perform the *chalitzah* ritual which releases her to remarry (*Deuteronomy* 25:5-10). In our times, levirate marriage has been prohibited by the Sages, so that the widow must perform *chalitzah*.]

"'I have a brother, but I do not know where he lives. After I am gone, go to the local Rav and give him the necessary information so that he can contact other communities in order to locate my brother, who will give you *chalitzah* and receive half of the estate.'

"That is exactly what happened. The local Rav sent messages to all the Jewish communities, and my father was identified as my uncle's brother. He had no money to travel to Apta, and his Rav lent it to him, expecting that he would repay him from the inheritance.

"When my father related this to my mother, she said, 'It is rare that a person can fulfill the mitzvah of *chalitzah*. Since Hashem has given you the opportunity to fulfill this rare mitzvah, you should do so only because it is a mitzvah and for no ulterior motive. I suggest that you do not take any of the estate.'

"My father agreed, but because my mother was afraid that he might not resist the temptation to take the inheritance, she made him promise that he would not take the money. He returned the travel money to the Rav, because he had no expectation that he would be able to repay it.

"My father trekked on foot several weeks until he reached Apta. He was shabbily dressed, and the widow gave him fine clothes so that he should appear respectable. The *chalitzah* ritual was performed. When he told the widow that he would not take any of the inheritance, she said that she did not want to keep what was not rightfully hers, and she donated his half of the estate to the coffers of the Apta community. My father left Apta, leaving the fine clothes.

"This caused an uproar in Heaven: a needy person had turned down a fortune in order to perform the mitzvah with no ulterior motive. At that time, my parents were childless, so the Heavenly tribunal rewarded them with a child. That is how I was born.

"Now you can understand why I requested a double wage when I came to Apta. I was not imposing on the community. Rather, I was taking that which had been donated to the community because of my father's actions. I have made a careful calculation, and over the years I have received an amount equal to that given to the community at that time. Therefore, I wish to return to my former town, Medzhibozh.

"However, I will always be remembered as the Rav of your community, the Rav of Apta."

Kankan HaKesef II

When Rebbe Elimelech went into his self-imposed exile, he came to the town of Chernovitz, and asked the *parnes* for permission to deliver a *derashah* in shul. The *parnes* refused, and when Rebbe Elimelech pleaded, he threw him out. The *parnes'* young son, Avner, said to his father, "Why don't you allow this man to deliver a *derashah*? He is obviously poor, and the people will give him a few coins."

The *parnes* relented and gave his permission. Rebbe Elimelech ascended the pulpit and began looking all around, but did not say a word. The people asked, "Why aren't you speaking? What is it that you are looking for?"

Rebbe Elimelech said, "I am looking for a trace of *yiras Shamayim*. All I see here are people who care only about themselves and have no interest in serving Hashem."

The people became irate and chased Rebbe Elimelech from the pulpit, threatening to beat him, and he ran for his life. After the crowd stopped pursuing him, Avner continued to follow him. He said to Rebbe Elimelech, "I know you are in need of money. Here, take this," and handed him a bag of coins.

Rebbe Elimelech said, "That is your father's money. You have no right to give it away."

Avner replied, "This is my allowance. I can do whatever I wish with it."

Rebbe Elimelech put his hand on Avner's head. "How shall I bless you?" he asked.

Avner said, "Bless me in any way you wish."

Rebbe Elimelech said, "I bless you that one day we shall be *mechutanim*.

Many years later, Avner's daughter married a grandson of the Rebbe of Apta, who was also a descendant of Rebbe Elimelech. When the Rebbe of Apta came to Chernovitz for the wedding, he sent for Avner.

"Tell me," he said, "by what virtue did you merit to become a *mechuten* with Rebbe Elimelech?"

"I don't know," Avner said. "I am only a simple Jew. I give *tzeddakah* and fulfill the mitzvah of *hachnassas orchim*.

"Those are certainly great mitzvos," the Rebbe of Apta said, "yet they are not enough to merit becoming a *mechuten* with Rebbe Elimelech, who was an angel rather than a mere human being. Tell me more, Reb Avner. Is there anything special you can recall doing?"

After a few moments, Avner said, "I remember that when I was young, a poor rabbi came to our town. The people chased him out because he chastised them. I felt pity for him, and I gave him whatever money I had."

"Can you describe this man?" the Rebbe of Apta asked. Avner then gave a precise description of the man.

The Rebbe of Apta excitedly jumped to his feet. "Yes, yes!" he said. "That was he! That was the Master!"

Avner said thoughtfully, "Come to think of it, he blessed me that we may one day become *mechutanim*."

The Rebbe of Apta said, "I am not at all surprised that Rebbe

Elimelech foresaw the future. What is remarkable is that he was so humble as to accept the money from a youngster."

A man from Apta was drafted into the army, which for a Jew was almost a death sentence. Not only was it impossible to obtain kosher food, but one also became the victim of anti-Semitic soldiers. One Friday, the Rebbe of Apta was resting in the bathhouse. Some leading community citizens were there as well, and the Rebbe impressed upon them the need to raise funds to buy this man's release.

The people agreed, but one person said, "Why is the Rebbe so intent on freeing this young man? If he won't be here, won't our city still be a city?"

Upon hearing this, the Rebbe paled. The Rebbe returned to his bath, while the man who had spoken got dressed and left for home. On the way home, he was gored by an ox.

The man's family, hearing that he had offended the Rebbe, went to apologize on his behalf, and met the Rebbe as he was leaving the bathhouse.

The Rebbe said, "Heaven forbid that I prayed for him to be punished! Furthermore, I was in the bathhouse and could not pray there. However, when he said, 'If he won't be here, won't our city still be a city?' the thought flashed through my mind, 'And if this man were not here, won't our city still be a city?' I promptly banished the thought from my mind. He was not punished because of my thought, but because he had said that this young man was superfluous. His own words punished him."

Sipurei Chassidim, Zevin

An eyewitness reported the following.

"The custom of the holy Rebbe was to have a *seudas Rosh Chodesh* [festive meal on the first day of the new month] with his chassidim. On *Rosh Chodesh Nissan*, he had the usual *seudah*, and spoke about the topic of the deaths of *tzaddikim*, saying that on the day a *tzaddik* dies, he is shown his reward, and he is pleased, as is said in *Ecclesiastes* 5:11, 'Sweet is the sleep of the laborer.' At the time of death, Hashem greets him with joy, as the *Zohar* says, 'When the time comes for the *neshamah* to depart from the *tzaddik*, it does not leave the body until the *Shechinah* reveals itself, and amidst the joy of the *Shechinah*, the *neshamah* leaves the body.' The Rebbe elaborated on this as well as on other quotations about the death of *tzaddikim*.

"After *Birchas HaMazon*, the Rebbe arose from his seat and his face was radiant as if aflame, verily like a Heavenly angel. He paced to and fro, and began speaking about the table. 'This pure table,' he said, 'will testify in the Heavenly world that I fulfilled the words of the Sages of the *Mishnah* —I ate with my company at this table, and I spoke words of Torah at it, and I did not speak, Heaven forbid, any idle talk. Also, that I was not, Heaven forbid, a glutton, and that I ate only for the health of my body, and that I did not eat grossly to fill my stomach like those people who eat and drink and make all their days festive.'

"Then he went over to the menorah, and said, 'The menorah will testify in the Heavenly world that by its light I studied Torah.' Then he took his *kiddush* goblet and said, 'This goblet will testify in the Heavenly world that I made *kiddush* and *havdalah* Shabbos and Yom Tov, to rectify its roots in the Heavenly world, and that I had all the proper *kavannos* to elicit the outpouring of *berachah* in all the worlds, and never had any alien thoughts, Heaven forbid.'

"Then the Rebbe went to the bookcase and raised his holy right hand toward Heaven, saying, 'All these *sefarim* will speak and give valid testimony before the Throne of Glory, that I studied with *kavannah* without a trace of vanity or ulterior motives, Heaven forbid, and I did not study them to serve as a way of earning a livelihood, but I studied them purely *lishmah* [for the sake of the mitzvah].'

"Then he went over to the *Aron Kodesh* [holy ark], opened it, and, extending his head into the *Aron Kodesh*, wept profusely, and said, as Moses did, that he is asking Hashem to grant him a gift of pure grace, even though *tzaddikim* can ask for the reward for their good deeds.

"When the Rebbe realized that his prayers were not being accepted and that the Heavenly decree that he should go to his eternal rest was irrevocable, he placed his hands on the holy *sefer Torah,* kissed it, and said, 'The holy *sefer Torah* will testify in the most high places that I respected it properly and that I read it without ulterior motives, and also that the reader of the Torah was a G-d-fearing man, and that I supervised his reading of the Torah on Shabbos, Yom Tov, Rosh Chodesh, and Mondays and Thursdays so that he should read it exactly according to our *mesorah* [tradition], and that when I was called to the Torah, I recited the *berachos* with intense *kavannah*. And the *Chumash* in which I studied will also testify before the Most High that every Friday afternoon I reviewed the *parashah*, reading the verses twice and the *targum* [Aramaic translation] once, and that I did not ignore any of the full words or those with missing letters, nor any of the musical notes, and I expounded on every verse of the Torah with the most profound hidden meanings.'

"Then he went to the doorposts of all the rooms and said, 'I fulfilled the mitzvah of the Torah to write the excerpts of *Shema* and the other portions as written in the Shulchan Aruch, and I affixed them to the doorposts, reciting the proper *berachah*, and I fulfilled the halachah to check the *mezzuzos* twice in seven years. And the *mezzuzos* will testify in the Heavenly world that I established times and moments to study Torah constantly, as the Sages said, "Just as the *mezzuzah* is permanently affixed to the doorpost, so shall you be permanerntly affixed to the *beis midrash*."'

"When he finished his holy words, he instructed the *chevrah kadisha* [the members of the burial society) to make his coffin from the table at which he ate.

"That month [on the 5th day of *Nissan*] the Heavenly angels triumphed over the mortals, and the Holy Ark [the Rebbe] was taken."

There is a mysterious story about the burial of the Rebbe of Apta, who had acquired a plot in the cemetery in Tiberias. The night that he died, a knocking was heard at the Volhynia *beis midrash* in Tiberias, and an announcement was heard: "Go out and escort the Rebbe of Apta to his eternal rest."

When the people went out, they saw a bier borne through the air, and they followed it to the cemetery, where it was lowered into the grave that the Rebbe of Apta had purchased. Yet the tombstone in Medzhibozh marks the resting place of the Rebbe of Apta.

~§ *Epilogue*

I cannot help but reflect on the nature of the relationship between these four *tzaddikim* and Rebbe Elimelech. His bequest of his powers to them bespeaks of a relationship as of a father to his children. This is the way it should be, because the Talmud says that if a person teaches Torah to the child of his fellow, the Torah considers it as if he were his own child (*Sanhedrin* 19b).

I assume that this is the way things were, that is, until recently. Just several decades ago, if you had asked my brother where he was learning, he would have answered, "By Reb Shloime," refering to Rav Shloime Heiman, Rosh Yeshivah of Mesifta Torah Vodaas. Another person would have said, "By Reb Ahron," and yet another person would have said, "By the Rav." The answer would have been the name of his Talmud teacher. Today, if you ask someone where he is learning, you will get the answer, "Brisk," or "Ponovezh," or "Lakewood," or "Baltimore." A *place*, not a *person*.

I cannot but conclude that the unique relationship between a teacher and a student no longer exists. This is not only unfortunate for the two of them alone, but it also has wider ramifications. Although the four *tzaddikim* whose lives are touched upon in this volume lived a great distance from one another, they maintained close spiritual and emotional contact. When the teacher was seen as a spiritual father, the students were spiritual brothers, and there was a bond between them as the children of one father. This bond does not exist when there is no spiritual father, only a geographic location. Perhaps if we are aware of it, we can restore the relationship that enables a teacher to bequeath his meritorious qualities to his students.